Praise for *Paying for Tomorrow: Maintaining Our Quality of Life*

Michael Curley urges us all to face the hard truth that, if you will the end, in this case a cleaner environment, you must will the means, specifically the necessity of paying for it. The good news is that Curley provides a roadmap on how to cost effectively achieve the goals of environmental protection and sustainability in ways that are both realistic and achievable. So in the end, his book is a very hopeful one.

—G. Tracy Mehan, III
Former Assistant Administrator for Water at U.S. EPA,
and Executive Director for Government Affairs,
American Water Works Association

It is widely understood that the task of restoring and protecting the quality of the environment has become steadily more complex and more urgent. Over recent decades, governments at all levels have approached this task with a growing portfolio of programs and regulations. Yet, even a cursory examination of environmental policy would suggest that it is designed to address two distinct problems: what to do and, with much less attention, how to pay for it. These two problems are by no means separate. In fact, they are deeply interrelated. Michael Curley, in accessible but still eloquent prose, demonstrates the consequences of ignoring this relationship. He also shows the potential for novel financing methods to improve the overall efficiency and effectiveness of environmental management. Curley has spent his career advocating for creative approaches to environmental finance. In this book, he presents a broad picture of what is known about better financing methods, and what is possible. This is critically important information if we are to meet present and future environmental challenges at least cost, financed in a way that is effective, fair, and protective of jobs, other resources, and social values.

— John J. Boland, Ph.D., P.E.
Professor Emeritus, Johns Hopkins University

Michael Curley has always been one of the most creative and influential thinkers in the field of environmental finance. This book is a continuation, and perhaps a culmination, of Michael's creative genius in this field. A must-read for anyone concerned with the future of our environment and how we are going to pay for the many initiatives that will be needed to maintain and improve it over future generations.

—Paul K. Marchetti, Ph.D.
Former Executive Director,
Pennsylvania Infrastructure Investment Authority (PENNVEST)

PAYING FOR TOMORROW: MAINTAINING OUR QUALITY OF LIFE

by Michael Curley

ENVIRONMENTAL LAW INSTITUTE
Washington, D.C.

Copyright © 2018 Environmental Law Institute
1730 M Street NW, Washington, DC 20036

Cover design by Davonne Flanagan.

Published June 2018.

Printed in the United States of America
ISBN 978-1-58576-193-7

Contents

About the Author v

Acknowledgements vii

Foreword ix

Introduction 1

Chapter 1: Why Tomorrow Is Different 5

Chapter 2: The Payment Question 11

Chapter 3: Affordability 27

Chapter 4: Subsidies 31

Chapter 5: Tariffs 37

Chapter 6: Financing Environmental Projects 43

Chapter 7: Credit Enhancement 47

Chapter 8: Old Water/New Water 61

Chapter 9: Old Air/New Air 75

Chapter 10: Resilience and Cybersecurity 81

Chapter 11: The Private Sector 101

Glossary 105

About the Author

Michael Curley is a lawyer and entrepreneur who has spent the majority of his career in project finance and the last 25 years in energy and environmental finance. Since 2013, he has been a Visiting Scholar at the Environmental Law Institute (ELI). He also serves on the Advisory Board of "Protect Our Power," a not-for-profit corporation created to defend the country's electric power grid from cyber attacks and electromagnetic pulses.

Mr. Curley has had a prolific writing career and is the author of several books, including *Fundamentals of Water Finance* (CRC Press 2016), *Finance Policy for Renewable Energy and a Sustainable Environment* (Taylor & Francis 2014) (translated into Chinese for the Central University for Finance & Economics), and *The Handbook of Project Finance for Water and Wastewater Systems* (Taylor & Francis 1993). He is a regulor contributor to the *Huffington Post* and is a member of the American Society of Journalists and Authors and the National Press Club. He has also published over 50 articles.

Mr. Curley has worked in 40 countries, primarily as the Senior Financial Advisor to the Office of International Affairs at the U.S. Environmental Protection Agency (EPA) and in the same capacity for the World Resources Institute. He has had extensive dealings with the World Bank, the Asian Development Bank, the European Bank for Reconstruction and Development, as well as the Organization for Economic Cooperation and Development. In 1990, Mr. Curley was appointed to the Environmental Financial Advisory Board at EPA, where he served for 21 years under four presidents.

Mr. Curley has also held several positions in state government. He served as Deputy Commissioner & General Counsel of the New York State Department of Economic Development, and then as President and CEO of the state's bank for economic development. He was also the General Counsel of the New York State Science & Technology Foundation, the state's venture capital agency. Prior to that, Mr. Curley served as Parliamentarian of the New York State Assembly and Associate Counsel to the Speaker. Mr Curley was also an Assistant to Rep. Richard D. McCarthy (D-N.Y.) in Washington, D.C. Mr. Curley was appointed to the Board of Directors of the United Nations Development Corporation by New York City Mayor Ed Koch.

Over the last 20 years, he has taught environmental & energy finance and law courses at Johns Hopkins University, George Washington University, and Vermont Law School. He founded the Environmental Finance Centers at the University of Maryland, Syracuse University, and Cleveland State University. He also served as Adjunct Professor of Banking & Finance at New York University teaching Venture Capital and Capital Markets.

In the early 1980s, he raised the venture capital for, founded, and served as president and CEO of the third municipal bond insurance company in the world and the first to insure economic development projects. The company had 28 employees when he sold it to a major international bank. Mr. Curley was also a partner in the celebrated New York City law firm of Shea & Gould.

Mr. Curely was also a member of the Board of the International Rural Water Association, where he built water and basic sanitation systems in El Salvador, Guatemala, and Honduras. He continued this work for several years privately in Honduras and Guatemala.

A prolific author, Mr. Curley also enjoys writing fiction. His first novel, a thriller entitled *YELLOWSTONE: Final Extinction*, was published in January 2016. He is currently working on a sequel novel entitled *The Calypso Virus*.

Acknowledgements

I want to mention some of the people whom I rely on for good advice and help as I did many times during the writing of this book. Each has always been unfailingly gracious and generous with advice and assistance.

First and foremost is my good friend of 30+ years, George Ames, who now runs the Clean Water State Revolving Fund (CWSRF) at the U.S. Environmental Protection Agency (EPA). Not only does George run the CWSRF, but he was part of a team of three who thought it up and drafted Title VI of the Clean Water Act (CWA), which authorizes it. The CWSRF is the single most successful environmental finance program on planet Earth. In his spare time over his 35+ year career at EPA, George also found the time to create the Environmental Financial Advisory Board as well as Environmental Finance Centers at nine major American universities. And while taking a short, voluntary leave of absence from EPA back in the late 1980s, he founded the Council of Infrastructure Financing Authorities, which is the national association of all 51 state CWSRFs.

Next, is my friend of 25+ years, Dr. John J. Boland, Professor Emeritus at the Johns Hopkins University. John is both a P.E. and a Ph.D. in Environmental Economics. He has taught at Hopkins for over 40 years, written over 150 articles, co-authored four books, and served six years on EPA's Environmental Financial Advisory Board. Whenever I write anything, I send it to John for a "sanity check" before I show it to anyone else.

Next, are three of my friends and colleagues at the Environmental Law Institute. First, Scott Fulton, the President. Next, John Pendergrass, Vice President for Programs and Publications. Third, Rachel Jean-Baptiste, Director of Communications & Publications. Rachel is the editor of this book. All three are very smart, very savvy, and great fun to work with.

Next, are my four serious mentors in the environmental finance game. The first is G. Tracy Mehan III, who is now the Executive Director of Government Relations at the American Water Works Association and was previously the Assistant Administrator for Water at EPA. Next, are my good friend, Adam Krantz, and his colleague, Chris Hornback. Adam is President and CEO of the National Association of Clean Water Agencies. Chris is Adam's deputy. The last mentor is Brent Fewell, founder and chair of the Earth & Water Law Group, who in addition to his stint as a senior executive in a major water company and as a partner in a major D.C. law firm, was also the principal deputy assistant administrator of EPA's Office of Water.

I also want to thank Jim Cunningham, whom I have known since we both worked for the New York State Department of Commerce in the 1970s. Jim has spent most of his career in one capacity or another in the electric power industry. Jim recently founded "Protect Our Power," a nonprofit that works to protect the U.S. electric power grid from cyber attacks. The electric grid is now the backbone of western civilization. It is essential to our quality of life. And it is very vulnerable to attack. If we don't pay to protect it, there may be no tomorrow!

Last but certainly not least, is my old friend, Joe Mysak, who probably knows more about U.S. public finance than anyone else on Earth. When I met Joe 35+ years ago, he was the publisher of *The Bond Buyer*. He is now the editor of the daily *Bloomberg Brief,* "Municipal Market." Along the way, he managed to write the *Encyclopedia of Municipal Bonds* and the *Handbook for Muni-Bond Issuers*.

To all of the above folks, a heartfelt thanks for all of your good advice and help.

Foreword

For the last 50 years, we have been spending huge sums of money on urban sewage to clean up our waterways and we have been imposing strict regulations on polluting businesses to keep our air clean. We still have to throw money at urban sewage but now agricultural runoff and stormwater are our #1 water problems, both of which we now need to pay for as well.

Who's going to pay for agricultural runoff? Farmers? Who's going to pay for an urban church to replace its parking lot with "green infrastructure? The pastor and the congregation? Do you know of any governor who's going to make either a farmer or the pastor of a church pay for these projects?

As jobs become more of a political issue, we can't keep putting stricter air pollution controls on businesses, which can just take their jobs and move to another state. We're going to have to start creating financial incentives for those businesses to stay.

So the first question is: who will pay for these new environmental challenges? Will they be affordable for the average citizen? Will there be subsidies? The next question is how will they pay for them? Can they finance them? What's the most cost-effective way to pay for them?

In addition to our old familiar problems with clean water and clean air, there are several new issues that we're just getting acquainted with. The first of these is global warming. We will need to pay to reduce the amount of greenhouse gases that we humans are pumping into the atmosphere each year. But in addition, we will have to pay to live with some of the inevitable consequences of global warming like rising sea levels and extreme weather events. Resilience, Adaptation, and Mitigation are the three new buzzwords for some of the strategies that we must embrace to survive global warming.

We're not used to thinking of rebuilding coastal cities after destructive hurricanes as a quality of life issue. But indeed it is. Just as much as dealing with asthma is when someone lives downwind of a huge chimney.

Another new quality of life issue is cybersecurity. What happens when the power goes out—for a long time? Will you have water? Will the toilets work? Will you be mobile? The U.S. power grid is highly vulnerable to vandals and terrorists. It is vulnerable to the weapons of foreign governments that are our enemies? And it is vulnerable to hackers of all sorts who can bring the cyber networks that we now all rely on to a complete halt.

So, that is what this book is all about. It is about what we are going to have to pay for in order to maintain our quality of life in the foreseeable future. And it is about the strategies we must employ to make sure that we use the most cost-effective and least expensive strategies to pay for them.

Introduction

Why is the concept "paying for tomorrow" important? There are several answers to this question.

First and foremost is the notion that quality of life is heavily influenced by the *quality* of our environment. Everyone seems to have a personal sense of environmental quality. In many cases, it can be a negative sense, which is what I experienced regarding a small city just south of Buffalo, New York, where I grew up, called Lackawanna. It is a name that means "stream that forks" in the language of the Lenni Lenape, an Indian tribe who inhabited a large swath of the mid-Atlantic around the Delaware River valley. The city was named not for a stream that forked, but actually for the company that owned the Lackawanna Steel plant, which moved its operations from the Scranton area to western New York in 1902.

The Lackawanna Steel plant, later the Bethlehem Steel plant, was built on the shores of Lake Erie just south of Buffalo. The city of Lackawanna was built inland from the plant. Unfortunately for the people who had to live there, "inland from the plant" meant "downwind" of the plant. This meant that the city of Lackawanna was blanketed daily with foul-smelling black smoke from the steel plant.

The ending to this Buffalo story is bittersweet. It is sweet because in 1983 the plant closed. Since then, the property has been rehabilitated into a pleasant lakeshore area. No more black smoke. But it is bitter because in its heyday the plant employed some 25,000 people. So, when looking out on the restored shoreline, you are reminded that there were once 25,000 people working there, all of whom are now gone. Later on in this book, you will read more about the connection between jobs and air pollution.

Regarding the issue of water pollution, there is another Buffalo story I'd like to share. Anyone who grew up in a city with heavy industry must have felt sick to their stomach, as I did, when they looked into their local river, which ran through the industrial part of town and carried off industrial waste. The water was brown and opaque. There were no fish and certainly there was no swimming! Thinking about Buffalo, it couldn't be more beautifully situated. It is at the end of Lake Erie, more than 250 miles east of Detroit. Looking west as far as the eye can see are Lake Erie and Canada. You would think that Buffalo's shoreline would have been populated by expensive high-rise apartment buildings to take advantage of the spectacular view. No, nothing of the sort. Beaches? None.

When I was a boy, my family would drive across the Peace Bridge into Canada, where we would swim in the water and enjoy their beautiful beaches. We also swam in Lake Erie. Back then, I could walk up to my neck in the lake and look down and see my toes! But things went downhill very quickly. By the time I was in law school, I would walk into Lake Erie and look down and I could barely see my shoulders—that's how polluted it was! Now, however, I can walk into Lake Erie and see my toes again. That is what the Clean Water Act (CWA) of 1972 did for us. In those days, urban sewage was the #1 source of water pollution. The CWA, as you will read later in this book, contained a "construction grant program." Once the act was passed, over the next 15 years the construction grant program pumped more than $70 billion into urban sewer systems, with about another $30 billion of local funds. The CWA was amended in 1987 to create the Clean Water State Revolving Fund (CWSRF), which pumped in another $125 billion. So since 1972, over $225 billion has been spent to clean up the urban sewage that was fouling Lake Erie and other major water bodies. And it worked!

Lots of people have their own stories. They have stories of their fathers cursing as they waited in traffic behind some stinking truck belching noxious fumes. Or they have stories of beaches that were closed because the water was too dirty to swim in.

The other, positive, side to these sad stories is the countless numbers of people who have wonderful memories and feelings about the environment. They have vivid recollections of spotless beaches or pristine mountain scenery with air that was perfectly clean and smelled fresh. Mountain streams that you could safely reach down and drink out of.

So, we all have feelings about our environment. We either want to keep the beauty and quality that we have, or, we want to change and clean up those areas of our environment that have been compromised. Environmental quality is inextricably bound up with our sense of the quality of our lives.

The first chapter of this book is entitled "Why Tomorrow Is Different." The answer is because many of the environmental battles that we fought over the past 50 years, we have actually won. But rather than resting on our laurels, we now face a new set of environmental challenges. They are different, as you will see. They need not be more difficult to solve. But they will be more expensive. This is easiest to see in the water sector. We have built elaborate systems to deliver safe drinking water and to clean up our sewage. We need to not only maintain this water infrastructure, but we must also replace much of it. To these costs we must add more funds to meet the new environmental challenges that we face. That is why it is imperative that we adopt the most cost-effective solutions to the problems we face now and in the future.

But there are some interesting aspects to these cost factors.

A few years ago when I was teaching at the Carey Business School at Johns Hopkins University, I had a student from Copenhagen in one of my classes. As an exercise, we determined that both his parents' apartment and mine were just about the same size. He found out how much they were paying for electricity and compared it to my bill. We learned that both I and his parents were paying about the same for power. But here's the rub. In Copenhagen, his parents were paying $0.37 per kilowatt hour (kwh). I was paying $0.09 per kwh. One way of looking at this, of course, is that they were paying over four times what I was paying for power. The other way of looking at this is that I was using over four times the power that his parents were using. Both ways of looking at this are correct. Denmark generates electricity from 100% renewable energy sources, much of it from offshore windmills. This, however, is very expensive. As a result, the Danes have learned how to build energy-efficient buildings and how to use electricity sparingly.

Here are some of the lessons we can learn from the exercise that my student and I undertook.

First, rising costs will promote conservation. This is a very good thing. The electricity is only $0.09 per kwh so why conserve? Why save energy?

Second, fossil fuels are cheap but they're dirty. They contribute to environmental degradation in so many ways. Not only do they make our air dirty, they even make our water dirty. As you will see, heavy metals and nitrogen from the burning of fossil fuels contaminate our lakes and rivers. This is most evident in pristine locales like the Adirondack Mountains.

Third, the price of these new—renewable—sources of energy will get cheaper the more they are used. It has been estimated that the price of solar power in 1977 was 100 times higher than it was in 2013. The more we use these new renewable energy sources, the cheaper they will become.

Finally, there are some new issues on the edge of our core environmental concerns that we will also have to pay for.

In addition to the fossil fuel/renewables evolution that we are already paying for that shapes our climate change efforts, we will have to pay for some of the inevitable consequences of global warming as well. We will sustain more extreme weather events and witness destructive sea-level rises. All of these will cost money in order to deal with them. There are some new government buzzwords like "resilience," "mitigation," and "adaptation" that describe the strategies for dealing with the consequences of global warming. These three new buzzwords, however, all come with their own price tags.

In addition, we need to pay to protect our electric power system from both natural and man-made perils that can leave major segments of our population without electricity. On September 20, 2017, Hurricane Maria struck Puerto Rico. By Christmas 2017, more than half the Puerto Rican homes were still without electric power. How would living without electric power for over four months affect the quality of your life? This could happen anywhere. And hurricanes are only one of many causes of electrical outages.

So, why should anyone be concerned about "paying for tomorrow"? The answer is because we're going to be paying for much more than we are now. And in order to minimize these expenses, we must design solutions that are the most cost effective.

We all need to know what we are going to be paying for and how much it is going to cost us. And we must not just be aware of but must actually employ the most cost-effective means of "paying for tomorrow" in order to preserve the quality of our lives.

Chapter 1—Why Tomorrow Is Different

The world started realizing the fragility of our natural surroundings—what we call "the environment"—in the middle of the last century.

On December 5, 1952, in London, there was an event called the "Great Smog of 1952" or the "Big Smoke." London had suffered from poor air quality since the 13th century. But with the advent of the Industrial Revolution, it became much worse. Industrial smoke, smoke from vehicles, and smoke from coal-burning furnaces shrouded the city almost constantly. In early December 1952, those pollutants became trapped by cold air close to the ground in what is called a "temperature inversion." The ensuing smog was so dense that it actually found its way indoors and caused the cancellation of some public events. Four thousand people were reported to have died in the four days the Great Smog hung like an incubus over London. The word "smog" itself is a portmanteau of "smoke" and "fog" that was coined early in the 20th century. Because the smog caused deep respiratory infections, which lasted months, the final death toll was estimated much later at about 12,000.

The United States got its own rude awakening on June 22, 1969, when the Cuyahoga River in Cleveland, Ohio, caught fire. That afternoon, oil-coated debris was ignited by sparks from a train passing along the river. Only $50,000 worth of damage was done to one railroad bridge, but the event caused a sensation in the press and captured the mind of the country. How could a river catch fire? As it turns out, the Cuyahoga River had caught fire some 13 times before. The event in 1969 wasn't even close to the worst incident. In 1952, a fire on the river caused some $1.3 million of damage. And in 1912, another Cuyahoga River fire killed five people.

The year after the 1969 Cuyahoga River fire, Congress passed the National Environmental Policy Act (NEPA), which was signed into law on January 1, 1970. NEPA is the archetypical environmental statute for the United States. In 1970, the Clean Air Act (CAA), which had been passed in 1963, was greatly expanded. And on December 2, 1970, President Richard M. Nixon founded the U.S. Environmental Protection Agency (EPA) by executive order. Two years later, Congress passed the CWA. The "age of environmental awareness" had officially begun.

In 1976, the Resource Conservation and Recovery Act (RCRA) was passed which governs the handling and disposal of solid and hazardous waste. Finally, in 1980, Congress passed the Comprehensive Environmental Response, Compensation, and Liability Act (CERCLA), which governs the cleanup of sites contaminated by toxic and hazardous wastes. It establishes a trust fund—called the "superfund"—to finance these efforts.

These five acts, NEPA, the CAA, the CWA, RCRA, and CERCLA, constitute the pillars of U.S. environmental law.

These laws were enacted in an era when urban sewage was the scourge of the nation's waterways. As I wrote in the Introduction, when I was a little boy growing up in Buffalo, New York, I could walk into Lake Erie up to my neck and look down and see my toes. Twenty years later, I could barely see my shoulders. Now, I can see my toes again. I credit this to the CWA.

As you know, one of the major provisions of the CWA was the construction grant program. With EPA's $70 billion and the local matching funds that the law required, the total spent on upgrading sewage treatment plants was about $100 billion. And that was in the 1970s when a billion dollars was a lot of money!

And so the sewage treatment plants in cities like Buffalo, Chicago, Cleveland, and Detroit were all upgraded. The quality of water in the Great Lakes improved tremendously.

The same sort of scenario took place with our nation's air. Back in the bad old days, our cities—much like London—were beset by emissions from coal-burning furnaces, which is how most homes were heated. Everyone has happy memories of the film "Mary Poppins." Some may remember the scene where Dick Van Dyke and Julie Andrews are singing "The Rooftops of London" and are literally dancing through a landscape that features thousands of smokestacks from home furnaces belching smoke. London was not alone. This was the condition of most major cities.

In addition to domestic coal furnaces, there were industrial furnaces. These not only burned coal, but wood, gas, or oil as well. They too were a major contributor to urban air pollution. Finally, and perhaps most importantly, there were automobiles. The emissions from cars and trucks were a major source of air pollution.

So, these are the issues that the CAA and the CWA addressed back in the early 1970s.

These laws were very successful. If Lake Erie is any example, our major water bodies are much cleaner. So is our air. Vehicular emissions have ceased to be a major problem. Of course, vehicular emissions can be dealt with at the source—manufacturing of automobiles. And, they can be dealt with by regulating the manufacturers. The cost of emission controls are buried in the overall price of a car.

If these statutes have been so successful at dealing with our pollution issues, then what is the problem now?

If urban sewage is no longer our #1 water pollution problem, then what is? The answer is twofold: agricultural runoff and stormwater. Agricultural runoff means the nutrients—mostly phosphorous and nitrogen—that are washed off farmland either by rain or by irrigation. Stormwater is mostly an urban problem. It becomes a problem in the areas where there are so many concrete or otherwise impermeable surfaces that do not absorb rainwater. Thus, when a serious rain event occurs, millions of gallons of rainwater course through cities into storm drains and then into a receiving water body. The water body not only gets the rainwater, but it also gets all of the pollutants that the rainwater picks up on its journey. This can mean garbage, animal feces, lawn fertilizers, other chemicals, and—above all—nitrogen from the atmosphere. As the rain passes through air that is loaded with nitrogen, it washes the nitrogen out and it winds up as a pollutant in the receiving water body.

Regarding air pollution, the new issues we face are far more subtle. In the past, if a factory or industrial facility emitted smoke, it had to have a permit. The permit spelled out precisely how much of each type of pollutant could be emitted into the air. In almost all cases, permits required a reduction in overall emissions. This meant new equipment to scrub the air before it was emitted. The equipment was expensive. Since it usually did not add one penny of productive capacity to any industrial facility, it was a pure financial burden on the owner who had to pay for the pollution abatement equipment out of his own pocket. The CWA provided billions of dollars to clean up water pollution. There was no comparable provision in the CAA. Of course there was a big difference in the causes of air and water pollution. The major cause of water pollution was us—the public—through publicly owned wastewater treatment facilities. The air pollution was caused by private companies. Nevertheless, there was no financial assistance program in place to aid the owner of an industrial facility in receiving his permit and also lowering his emissions.

This situation is getting new scrutiny. Fifty years ago, the concept of jobs and economic development was a poor stepchild of government. In those days, few, if any, governments had offices or departments of economic development. Today, it is one of the major government issues with equivalent offices. And so, nowadays, local governments have to be careful about imposing costly air pollution control requirements on industries. Some of those industries might just pick up and head for a less zealous jurisdiction. If so, the community loses all of those valuable jobs.

The other new game in the air business involves climate change, global warming, and GHGs. This all has to do with the earth getting hotter. Most people know that there have been several ice ages. These are periods when the earth cools off and snow and ice cover large areas. Between the ice ages, the earth warms up. That is what is happening now. The earth is naturally warming.

To this, however, are added anthropogenic GHGs. These are chemicals that trap the sun's heat in the atmosphere and accelerate the warming of the planet. We humans contribute about 30 billion tons a year of carbon dioxide (CO_2), which is a major GHG. By planetary standards, this isn't very much. But these gases remain in the atmosphere, thus their effect is cumulative.

Most of the CO_2 that we contribute comes from the burning of fossil fuels at electric power-generating stations. The quantity of GHGs emitted by power plants is regulated by the states. The impact of these regulations—like the installation of air scrubbers—is reflected in our utility bills. As the cost of burning fossil fuels rises, however, the cost of renewable energy, such as solar and wind power is getting cheaper.

In the Introduction, I recounted an incident with one of my students from Copenhagen. Denmark gets the majority of its power from wind. He and I compared the cost of home energy between his parents' home in Copenhagen and my apartment in Maryland. We were both actually paying about the same amount of money. But in Maryland, I was paying $0.09 per kwh. In Copenhagen, his parents were paying $0.37 per kwh. The cost of power in Denmark was four times higher than in Maryland! Or to put it into a much more telling light, I was using over four times the power that my student's parents were using!

There are two points here. The more we use renewable energy, the less it will cost. The second point is even more important: conservation! The student's parents were using much less power than I was. This is the way of the future. In the air business we have to incentivize the conservation of energy

Chapter 1: Why Tomorrow Is Different

and the use of renewables. That is what we will be "paying for tomorrow" on the air side of our environmental equation.

On the water side, we will be paying to clean up agricultural runoff and to mitigate the impact of pollution-laden stormwater on our harbors, lakes, and rivers. This will bring many changes.

It might cost a farmer $50,000 to build a two-acre constructed wetland on his property to trap the runoff from his fields. But who is going to pay for this? The farmer? I doubt there is any governor or state legislature that would even consider forcing a farmer to spend $50,000 out of his own pocket for a pollution abatement project.

On the stormwater side, take the case of an urban church with a two-acre concrete parking lot. The concrete is impermeable, so the rain just glances off it and hurdles to the nearest drain. The cost of replacing the concrete with permeable pavement would be about $50,000. Who's going to pay for it? The congregation? I doubt there is any mayor or governor in the country who would pick up his phone and tell the pastor of a church to take the money out of the collection plate to pay for his stormwater problems.

No, we are going to have to devise new financial strategies to deal with the farmer and the pastor. This won't be easy. At present, we have neither the financial nor the operational structures to deal with these situations.

The CWSRF has provided over $125 billion of financial assistance to over 36,000 projects. Much like its predecessor, the construction grant program, 96% of the CWSRF's funds have gone to sewage treatment plants. The CWSRF program is well suited to writing multimillion dollar checks for sewage plant upgrades, but they have little experience with $50,000 projects on farms or church properties. And they certainly can't deal with the question of whether the farmer or the pastor should actually pay for these projects.

So, that is what "paying for tomorrow" is all about. It is about energy conservation and renewables as well as protecting jobs. It is about agricultural runoff and stormwater—the farmer and the pastor. As in the Danish example, we might wind up paying relatively the same amount of money, but "paying for tomorrow" will indeed be different.

Chapter 2—The Payment Question

When urban sewage was the number one source of water pollution, the payment question was easy. The state would issue each sewer authority a national pollutant discharge elimination system (NPDES) permit, which would specify exactly how much of each type of pollutant they were allowed to discharge into their receiving water body. If the agency needed to install new equipment to meet these requirements, then they would simply buy what they needed. From 1972 to 1987, they could get a construction grant from EPA to pay for a majority of the cost. After 1987, they could borrow money inexpensively from the CWSRF.

During the construction grant period, who paid the local share of the cost? The ratepayers did.

Since 1987, who repays the loan that the authority borrows from the CWSRF? The ratepayers do.

Why? Well, every time someone went to a lavatory and flushed a toilet in the authority's service area, it was they who were the source of the sewage that the authority was treating. So, the authority's ratepayers were paying for their own pollution.

Agricultural runoff is pollution caused by farms. It comes from untreated animal waste and it also comes from chemicals, mostly fertilizers, which are added to the soil to make crops grow better. The farms and the farmers are the source of this pollution. So, what is the difference between the pollution caused by the farmer and the pollution caused by the sewer authority's ratepayers? *Qualitatively*, there is not much difference. *Quantitatively*, there is all the difference in the world. On the pollution side, we humans don't produce that much waste. Farms, especially large farms, produce prodigious amounts of pollutants, which are also called nutrients.

The same is true on the money side. The annual payment on a low cost CWSRF loan to upgrade a treatment plant may cost many thousands of dollars. But the authority probably has tens of thousands—if not hundreds of thousands—of ratepayers. So, dividing up the annual payment and spreading it over a huge base of ratepayers does not amount to much of an increase

11

in the individual ratepayer's sewer bill. They might complain about it at public hearings, but it is never really so much as to break any homeowner's bank.

Let's take an example of a $100,000 upgrade to a sewage treatment plant caused by an amendment to their NPDES permit. The amendment will require removing X amount of nutrients from the plant's effluent. The required equipment will cost about $100,000.

A typical low-cost CWSRF loan of $100,000 might require an annual payment of $5,000. Let us say that the sewer authority has 10,000 ratepayers. That means it will cost each ratepayer $0.50 per year to pay for the required upgrade. Definitely not going to break any ratepayer's bank.

Now let us say that an upstream farmer can remove two times the amount of nutrients by building a constructed wetland to catch the runoff from his fields. The cost of the constructed wetland would be about $50,000.

So the constructed wetland would remove twice the amount of nutrients at half the cost. The farmer too could get a low-cost loan from the CWSRF. The debt service payment on such a loan would be about $2,500 a year.

I think you know where this example is going.

The problem here—the payment question—is that the farmer must pay the entire $2,500 each year out of his own pocket to achieve a better result than the sewer authority whose customers only have to pay $0.50 each.

Now, the sewer authority has an NPDES permit. They are regulated by law. They have no choice but to take some action to comply with their permit requirements.

On the other hand, there is no legal authority to require the farmer to do anything. He can simply go on polluting. This sounds like an ugly choice: keep polluting or pay $2,500 a year for the next 20 years. But in fact, that is the way things are. And that is why "paying for tomorrow" has to be different.

Putting it a slightly different way, what governor is going to tell a farmer that he has to undertake a $50,000 project and pay for it out of his own pocket? What state is going to force farmers to reduce their runoff at their own expense?

The same situation is true with stormwater. The less rainwater a parcel of property absorbs, the more it exacerbates the urban stormwater problem. If the rainwater has no place to go, it heads for the nearest sewer or conduit where it joins countless more gallons of rainwater which carries all of the pollutants from lawn fertilizer to animal waste to roadside garbage into the river or lake that receives the community's excess rain.

Chapter 2: The Payment Question

Properties that are impermeable create the worst stormwater problems. There are, however, new ways of dealing with impermeable land. One solution is using "green infrastructure." Green infrastructure is basically replacing concrete and cement with vegetation that absorbs rain as it falls. Another strategy—one that can be used for parking lots—is permeable pavement. This is pavement that allows rain to percolate underground to the earth below the pavement.

All of this said, when it comes to paying for green infrastructure, we have the same problem that we have on the farm: much of it needs to be on private land. That said, there are no NPDES permits that regulate stormwater on private land. There are finance programs—the same ones available to farmers—but they are loan programs. And the loans must be paid back. And so, the same question arises: who is going to pay for the green infrastructure on private property? The owner?

Again, putting it a different way, what governor or mayor is going to tell the pastor of a large urban church that he must tear up his concrete parking lot and replace it with, say, $50,000 of permeable pavement? And that he must take the money to pay for the permeable pavement out of the Sunday collection plate? No mayor I know would ask a pastor to do that!

The point here is that "paying for tomorrow" is going to be different than paying for today, or at least, paying for the past.

So how is "paying for tomorrow" going to be different? Well, different people will be paying for tomorrow.

Stormwater is turning out to be a special case. So we will deal with it in a chapter later in this book. So, to continue, let's start with agricultural runoff.

Right now, there are five possible sources of payment for loans, other than by the farmer himself, for projects such as constructed wetlands on farm properties.

They are:

1. By the downstream customers and ratepayers of the sewer authority. For lack of better terminology, we call this process "adoption."
2. By the state itself. The state's CWSRF actually absorbs or "eats" the cost of the upstream project. This process is called "sponsorship."
3. By a few of us. We are not trying to be coy here. This refers to "nutrient credit trading" where those few people who have NPDES permit problems and need nutrient credits actually buy them from the farmer who undertakes the project and owns the credits.
4. By many of us. This is where fees/charges are created and implemented on a regional, usually a watershed, basis.

5. By all of us. This is where there is a statewide fee or charge that is applicable to all residents and businesses.

New Payment Structure #1: "Adoption"

The first source of payments is the folks downstream who are the ratepayers of the sewer authority. For lack of better terminology, we call this "adoption."

How do ratepayers, say, 20 miles downstream wind up paying for the farmer to build a constructed wetland? To begin with, our convenient example makes perfect sense for them to do so. They will be removing twice as many nutrients at half the cost. Certainly makes sense.[1]

This business of having downstream ratepayers pay for upstream agricultural runoff projects is rare today. A major reason for this is numbers. How do you count the nutrients? How do you actually know that the constructed wetlands project will remove two times the nutrients?

There is a lot of science on this subject, but unfortunately there isn't a lot of consensus. There are no axioms. You can't say that a two-acre constructed wetland "will remove 50,000 pounds (lbs.) of nitrogen a year," for example. If you stop and think about it, this also makes sense. The amount of nutrient removal depends on many factors. What is being grown on the adjacent land where the runoff is coming from it? How much fertilizer does the farmer use? What are the weather considerations? Rain drives runoff, so how much does it rain every year?

As you can imagine, estimating the nutrient reduction needs human intervention. And, to a very large degree, it is subjective. For this reason, scientists are loathe to put precise numbers on the amount of nutrients removed.

The saving grace is the word "precise" in the last sentence. It isn't absolutely necessary to have a precise amount of nutrients; it is only necessary to convince the state environmental regulators that it is enough to solve the problem. For example, a sewer authority might identify an upstream farm where a constructed wetland could easily be built. Its own scientists might estimate that such a wetland would remove X amount of nutrients. Let's say that this X amount of nutrients is more than enough to satisfy the new requirement on the sewer authority's NPDES permit. And, also, that the construction of a wetland would be cheaper than the alternative of making an upgrade to their sewer plant.

---

1. Iowa had a state-law problem that appeared to limit sewer authority payments for projects within the geographic bounds of the authority. This was overcome with a brief amendment to the appropriate state statute.

In this case, the sewer authority would propose to the environmental regulators that the sewer authority would pay for the construction of the wetland instead of upgrading their sewage plant. They would probably invite the regulators (or their staff scientists) to inspect the wetland site.

Once the sewer authority had the agreement of the state regulators that the wetland would satisfy the new requirements of their permit, they could then make a deal with the farmer and go ahead and build the wetland.

As you can see, this is a hit or miss process. It is not widely done. We refer to this as an "adoption" project because the downstream sewer authority "adopts" the upstream constructed wetland project and passes the cost along to their ratepayers.

Remember from the discussion above that doing this achieves two times the necessary nutrient reduction at half the cost. So, in our above example, with a low-cost loan for the $50,000 upstream constructed wetland project, our 10,000 downstream ratepayers wind up paying $2,500 per year, which is $0.25 per household per year. This is the smart way to "pay for tomorrow."

New Payment Structure #2: "Sponsorship"

As you know, loans to sewer systems are very straightforward. They are repaid out of the sewer rates charged to usually thousands of customers. Nonpoint source projects, on the other hand, have no ratepayers. They are most often on private land. They often have no readily available source of repayment other than out of a farmer's own pocket.

In the late 1990s, the state of Ohio began to address this problem with a concept they call "sponsorship." Sponsorship programs were developed by the state of Ohio's EPA in conjunction with the Ohio Water Development Authority, which manages the CWSRF. Since Ohio created its program, Delaware, Idaho, Iowa, and Oregon, through their respective CWSRFs, have followed suit. Many other states are now considering developing such programs.

A sponsorship program looks very much like a grant program. But it isn't. It is actually a loan to a sponsor who adds it on to one of its own projects and pays off the loan for both projects at a much lower rate of interest that actually saves the sponsor a little money.

Here is a good example of a sponsorship project from the state of Iowa. Oddly enough, it deals with a stormwater problem, not an agricultural runoff problem.

In 2014, the Sioux City sewer system applied to the CWSRF to borrow $14.4 million to modernize some of its facilities. At the same time Sioux City was vexed by the water quality of a stream that ran right through town. The problem dealt with the eroding banks of the Ravine Park waterway that polluted the water before it entered Sioux City proper. Ravine Park was "characterized by steep, eroded gullies." What was needed was a project to shore up these gullies and stream banks to prevent the erosion, which would reduce the pollution coming downstream into Sioux City. Every time it rained, there was a torrent of muddy water pushing its way through town. The state did some engineering work and estimated that it would cost $1.4 million to stabilize the banks and get rid of the problem. But who would undertake the project? How would it get paid for? Nobody knew.

The state went to the Sioux City sewer system and they told them that the city could get a 2% (subsidized) loan for $14.4 million for 20 years, which would cost them $880,657 per year or they could agree to "sponsor" (pay for) the stream-bed project too, in which case the state revolving fund (SRF) would give them a $15.8 million loan[2] for 20 years at 1.03%, which would cost them $878,209! Two projects for the price of one! And actually a modest savings!

The reduced interest rate serves as a "carrot" for the wastewater utility to "sponsor" the upstream project. The cost of the watershed project is paid through savings realized from the reduced loan interest rate. The result is that two beneficial wastewater management projects with triple bottomline benefits get done for about the same cost as one traditional wastewater project alone.

Funds in the CWSRF come from three sources: (1) annual federal capitalization grants; (2) state matching funds at a 1:5 ratio; and (3) interest earned on the loans it makes, as well as temporary investments. So, the people of Iowa own these funds. And when they choose to subsidize projects, including sponsorship projects, the CWSRF is actually losing money.

How much can sponsorship projects be subsidized? Would the Ravine Park sponsorship project work if it were, say, $3 million. The answer is no. Here is some math.

If the market interest rate were 4% then most state CWSRFs would make their subsidized interest rate loans in the 2% range. Using a $10 million project as the "main" project, how much of a sponsored project can the CWSRF afford to finance? Well, the annual payment on the "main" project itself for

---

2. The original $14.4 million for the modernization project plus $1.4 million for the "sponsored" stream stabilization project equals $15.8 million.

20 years at 2% would be: $611,567. If we added a $1 million sponsored project, then it would be an $11 million loan. So, let's drop the interest rate to 1% and see what happens. The annual payment on a 20-year loan of $11 million at 1% would be $609,568. So, it works when the sponsored project is 10% of the size of the main project.

But what if the sponsored project were $2 million, or 20% of the size of the main project? Then the total loan would have to be $12 million. Would the sponsorship work at this level? No, not without additional subsidy from the CWSRF. Clearly the SRF would have to reduce the interest rate even further. To what level would the SRF have to reduce the interest rate to make it work? Well the answer is that the interest rate would have to be about 0.1%, which is one-tenth of 1%. To be exact, the annual payment on a $12 million loan for 20 years at 0.1% interest is $606,319. So it works at the 20% level, but only with the additional subsidy from the CWSRF.

In other words, sponsorship projects work when the sponsored project is 20%, or less, of the main project. And they can be an invaluable tool for paying for upstream problems, like agricultural runoff projects, which otherwise would not get done.

The beauty of CWSRF sponsorship programs is that they integrate two highly complementary approaches to water management—traditional treatment and upstream nonpoint source treatment—into a single loan repaid by water rates.

So, who pays for the CWSRF sponsorship programs? The answer is: the citizens of the state where the sponsorship project takes place. But they "pay" for it not as a cash outlay; rather they pay for it by forgoing the higher rate of interest. The CWSRF, which the citizens "own," doesn't make as much money as it could. In the above examples, a 2% interest rate was reduced to about 1%. So, the CWSRF didn't earn as much as it could have with a regular loan.

Thus, the key to the success of CWSRF sponsorship programs is the lower, or subsidized, interest rate. By subsidizing CWSRF loans, states decide to trade some CWSRF interest income for the clean water and other community benefits provided by sponsored projects.

Needless to say, the sponsorship program cannot be expanded infinitely. Every time a CWSRF does a sponsorship project they are losing money for the next 20 years. They can't do this forever. Both Iowa and Ohio set precise annual limits on the amount of sponsorship projects they will do. So, "sponsorship" is not a permanent answer to the payment question, but at the moment, it is a major player.

New Payment Structure #3: "Nutrient Credit Trading"

Nutrient trading is an excellent idea. Mechanically, it is very much like "adoption." It, however, envisions a much more sophisticated system. "Adoption," as you read, is very subjective and is hit or miss. Nutrient trading implies a system where nutrient credits are well known, well understood, and, above all, countable.

Nutrient credit trading has a distinctly technical side. It involves quantifying nutrients that pollute water into "credits." This task must be undertaken by environmental scientists who work for the state.

There are the usual two sides to the nutrient credit trading equation: those who can create credits and those who either need them, outright (like a developer, as you will read) or are willing to pay for them because they just want the benefit.

Think of a farmer who will plant a few rows of nitrogen-absorbing trees along the banks of the stream that runs across his property. The farmer actively works his field. No matter how careful he is dosing his fields with fertilizer, there is always some that runs off when it rains and winds up in the stream, which ultimately winds up in someone's drinking water intake downstream. The trees, which the farmer plants, absorb the nitrogen, preventing it from going downstream.

The trees are going to cost the farmer $100,000 to plant. He is not thrilled about paying for this out of his own pocket. Planting the trees isn't going to improve his crop yield and put more money in his pocket. So, he consults with representatives of his conservation district who tell him about the nutrient credits he could earn. They suggest he invite out to his farm the scientists from the state EPA to determine how many credits he could earn. The conservation district people also tell him about low cost loans available through a program that the district manages on behalf of the state CWSRF. So the farmer investigates the situation.

The scientists come out, look over the proposed project, look at the locations where the trees will be planted and conclude that the farmer could earn 10,000 nutrient credits for undertaking the project to plant the trees. The farmer also learns that he can get a $100,000 loan from the CWSRF through the program where they partner with the conservation district. The loan would be at a subsidized rate of 2% and would have a 20-year term. The farmer does the math and sees that he would owe the CWSRF $6,116 per year in annual payments.

Chapter 2: The Payment Question

In the course of working with the CWSRF, the farmer learns that the state has organized a nutrient credit trading program. Upon further investigation, he learns that there is a developer downstream who wants to build a subdivision. But the sewage treatment plant that serves his proposed development is maxed out on its NPDES permit. The only way the publicly owned treatment work (POTW) can increase its capacity is if it gets credits from somewhere. So, the sewer authority tells the developer to go out and buy 15,000 nutrient credits and then they'll hook up his new subdivision to their POTW. He has no choice.

Through the auspices of the CWSRF, the farmer puts his 10,000 credits on the market for $0.70 apiece. That would give him $7,000 per year, and his annual payment to the CWSRF is only $6,116. So, the farmer would actually make a small profit if he could sell the credits for, say, 70 cents apiece.

The developer does his own math and determines that he will pay up to $6,000 a year, or $0.60 per credit. The developer finds out about the farmer's 10,000 credits being offered at 70 cents each through the CWSRF. The developer needs 15,000, but the farmer's 10,000 credits is a very good start.

Eventually, again, with the assistance of the CWSRF, the farmer and the developer reach agreement on a price of $0.65 per credit. So, again, the farmer makes a small profit and the developer gets the permit approvals he needs from the state so he can complete his subdivision project.

Recall the example above in the discussion about adoption. In that case, the engineers for the sewer authority thought it would be less expensive to pay a farmer to build a constructed wetland than to upgrade their treatment plant. So, they went to the state regulators and got them to agree that the reduction in nutrients caused by the development of a constructed wetland would satisfy their NPDES permit requirements.

In the case of nutrient trading, it would probably be the other way around. Here a farmer might learn that constructed wetlands were important in the reduction of nutrients. He might think that a couple of his acres that weren't much good for crops could easily be turned into a constructed wetland. He would then call in a scientist from the state environmental agency to estimate the nutrient reduction that would result from his proposed constructed wetland. The scientist would tell him that such a wetland would produce X amount of nutrient credits.

The farmer would then estimate the cost of construction and what rate and term he could get on a low-cost loan from his CWSRF. He would then calculate his annual cost.

Next the farmer would check out the going rate that sewer authorities, developers, and others who were active buyers in the nutrient credit market would pay per credit.

If the numbers made sense to the farmer, he would put his X amount of nutrient credits on the market and, assuming he is successful, he will have achieved a nutrient credit trade.

As you can see, the important element here—the one that distinguishes it from some type of adoption—is the numbers, the metrics. The nutrient reduction here isn't just something in the mind of a scientist or a state regulator. In the case of a real nutrient credit trading market, the credits are a commodity. They are known amounts. They are no longer subjective. They are very objective: 50,000 lbs. of nitrogen per year; 10,000 lbs. of phosphorus. They are numbers like these. So, if a sewer authority gets a revision in its NPDES permit that requires it to remove, say, another 100,000 lbs. of the nutrients which they estimate would cost $20,000 per year, they could instead buy a farmer's 50,000 lbs. of nutrient reduction for anything less than $10,000 per year and they would be about 50% of the way to their goal and saving money in the process.

That's how nutrient credit trading is supposed to work. At least a simplified version of how it should work.

So, why doesn't it work?

The answer again begins with the metrics, the numbers. There are no scientists—whether independent or employees of the state—whom the farmer can call who will give him an ironclad estimate of the amount of nutrients his propose wetland would absorb. No scientist is going to say 50,000 lbs. or 10,000 lbs. or anything else.

But let's say that our farmer lucks upon a really bold independent scientist who actually agrees to the estimate of 50,000 lbs. of nutrients and puts it in writing. What then?

Next, the farmer calls in an engineer who can estimate not only the cost of construction, but also the annual maintenance cost. That's the easy part, but, of course, the engineer must be paid and the farmer is the only one who can do that.

Next, the farmer contacts the CWSRF and gets their rates and terms. So now he knows what his annual payment will be on the project.

Next, the farmer makes a call to whichever agency managed the nutrient credit program and finds out what the going rate is that buyers are paying for credits.

The problem is that there is no one to call.

Chapter 2: The Payment Question

As of this writing, the Government Accountability Office (GAO) has just issued a study on nutrient trading entitled: "Water Pollution, Some States Have Programs to Help Address Nutrient Pollution, but Use Has Been Limited." To say that "use has been limited" is an understatement. The GAO found that only 11 states have nutrient credit trading programs at all, and that only 3 of the states have any significant trading activity: Connecticut, Pennsylvania, and Virginia. Of these three, Connecticut's and Virginia's programs are limited to "point-to-point," which means that the only parties who are trading are those with point sources of pollution who have NPDES permits. So, let's say that the city of X Sewer Authority is removing 100,000 lbs. of nitrogen with their equipment, but are only required by their NPDES permit to remove 50,000 lbs. In this case, they are free to sell the extra 50,000 lbs. And, so the city of Y Sewer Authority has a permit that requires them to remove 150,000 lbs. of nutrients, but their current equipment can only remove 100,000 lbs. In this case, city of Y Sewer Authority could buy city of X Sewer Authority's extra 50,000 lbs. of nutrients instead of upgrading its plant. The two sewer authorities could "trade nutrient credits."

The GAO found that only one state, Pennsylvania, has a nutrient credit trading program that applies to farms, etc., with the likes of nonpoint source agricultural runoff. It is managed by a state agency called PennVest, which also manages their CWSRF. And even Pennsylvania's program is far from robust. They currently have only four auctions a year, but there are only a handful of trades at each auction.

So, what is the future of nutrient trading?

Probably, the CWSRFs are going to have to intervene. Someone with money and a reason for wanting to create a nutrient credit trading system. The CWSRFs have both. Using our example, the CWSRF could buy the nutrient credits from the farmer. They could inventory these credits, so that both buyers and sellers would be able to see the size of the market. They could then sell them to willing buyers as Pennsylvania does now. To the extent that the price the CWSRF gets for the credits exceeds what would have been the debt service on a loan to the farmer, then that is good and thus the CWSRF will have more money to work with. If not, well, at least they got rid of the polluting nutrients.

So, nutrient credit trading is a program for tomorrow.

New Payment Structure #4: "Regional Funds"

This new payment structure and the next one, New Payment Structure #5: "Statewide Funds," are birds of the same feather. They are both "funds." The regional one is just a diminutive version of the statewide one.

What we are talking about here are funds that in no way are connected to sewer authorities. They are independent funds.

These independent funds are created by one or another unit of government or government agency. The money in these funds comes from fees, charges, or taxes that are imposed by the government or agency. They have, or should have, several very important characteristics.

First of all, they should plainly say what the money is going to be used for. Maryland has a statewide fund called the Bay Restoration Fund, where the money comes from the Bay Restoration Fee, which is actually a tax. Everyone in Maryland is familiar with the Chesapeake Bay, the nation's largest estuary. So, the Bay Restoration Fee makes perfect sense to them. They may not like paying it, but they certainly understand why they are doing so. After all, who doesn't want a clean Bay? So what if it costs a few bucks a month!

Another state in the Midwest was thinking of creating a statewide fund and calling it the "state clean water fund." Good for them. Good name.

Another state was considering creating a clean water fund, but they were thinking of funding it with a one penny increase in their sales tax. Bad idea. People will complain about it without understanding its underlying purpose—clean water. No one is going to say: "Oh, well, the extra penny is for a good purpose." Here the good purpose is lost because it's not in the name of the tax/fee.

The second important characteristic is that the fee should be as broad based as possible. Everyone pollutes. Everyone enjoys the benefits of clean water. So, everyone should pay. It's not just industries and not just farms and farmers; it's all of us.

So, fees should be payable by as many individuals, businesses, and other organizations as possible.

The third important characteristic is that the fee should be reasonable. It should not be painful for the public to pay.

There are almost no regional funds in the United States. In 2005, the city of Raleigh started a program to protect the Upper Neuse River watershed. They funded it initially with a budget allocation of $500,000 a year. Six years later they created a "watershed protection fee," which they charged to the customers of its water utility. The fee was 1 cent per 100 gallons of water. It

Chapter 2: The Payment Question   23

cost the average homeowner about 40 cents a month. Definitely didn't break any household budgets. Raleigh's fee brings in about $1.8 million per year.

The city of Durham also created its own fund, also based on water bills. They charged considerably more than Raleigh. Durham charged 1 cent per cubic foot of water. A cubic foot of water is only about 7.5 gallons. Assuming the Durham folks use the same amount of water as do the Raleigh people, then this fee would amount to about $6 a month. Again, not a budget buster.

The fourth important characteristic is that the money should not be piddled away. This might seem silly at first glance; but it isn't. The money collected each year should be used to pay debt service on bonds or other debt incurred to fund projects that need to be done today, not 30 years from now. It should not be used to put a nickel here and a dime there into pet projects. The managers of these funds should determine which pollution control projects are critical and need to be undertaken today, not 30 years from now.

The $1.8 million that Raleigh collects can support about $30 million of bonds issued to fund pollution control projects. In addition to getting critical projects done now and quickly, there is also the economic argument that money loses value over time because of inflation. And inflation is very real. If something costs $1 today, using a 3% annual inflation rate, you will have to have $2.42 to pay for it in 2047. And remember, the public doesn't like paying fees. So, every time you have to increase them—even just to keep up with inflation—you will feel the displeasure of those who must pay.

So, don't collect your $1.8 million a year and sit around waiting for over 12 years to have the $20 million needed for a critical project. Get that project done today. Use the fees to pay debt service on a $20 million bond to pay for it.

The fifth and final important characteristic of environmental fees is to make uses or purposes of the fund as broad as possible. They should be used to reduce any kind of pollution. Not just agricultural runoff. Not effluent from POTWs. Not just stormwater. Any form of water pollution!

What you see as a major problem today might need help from another area tomorrow. For example, stormwater problems might easily be exacerbated by agricultural runoff from upstream areas. You need to have funds that are versatile and, in this case, can attack both sources of pollution.

New Payment Structure #5: "Statewide Funds"

Statewide funds have all of the important characteristics that regional funds have. They are just broader based, which, of course, is one of the important characteristics of any environmental fee.

As of this writing, there is only one statewide fund. As noted above, it is Maryland's "Bay Restoration Fee."

As noted above, when the people of Maryland pay the Bay Restoration Fee, they know exactly where the money is going—to their beloved Chesapeake Bay.

It was originally based on the number of toilets in a building. The local news media reinforced the purpose of the Bay Restoration Fee by referring to it as the "flush tax." Now, that's what everyone in Maryland, except the politicians, call it!

The story goes that some good soul determined that the average single-family home has something like 2.3 or 2.8 toilets. That became the metric for the fee. That number became the equivalent residential unit (ERU). So each single-family home was charged for one ERU. For other buildings, the state estimated how many ERUs there were. So, for example, a small office building might have three or four ERUs, which means that they would pay three or four times what a single-family household would pay.

The flush tax is very reasonable. In 2004, when it was created, it was $2.50 per month per ERU. In 2012, the flush tax was doubled to $5 per month per ERU, with barely a whimper from the public.

The flush tax is used to pay debt service on bonds issued to pay for projects that needed doing immediately, not in the distant future. Originally it was used to pay debt service on bonds issued to fund enhanced nutrient removal (ENR) equipment on the state's largest POTWs. Although this purpose is unfortunately narrow, the state is slowly expanding the purposes for which the flush tax can be used.

So, the Maryland flush tax is truly ingenious and deserves emulation by other states. There is only one problem with the whole flush tax scenario. The Maryland Constitution limits the pledging of tax revenues to 15 years. This means that the bonds issued to fund the ENR projects can only have terms of 15 years. This is seriously unfortunate. In public finance, the rule is that bonds should be issued for terms equal to the service lives of the assets they are financing. Almost all ENR equipment has service lives of 30+ years. So, the bonds should have been issued for 30 years instead of 15. Maryland is the only state with this restrictive 15-year rule. The Maryland General Assembly has, thus far, refused to amend their constitution

What's the difference? About 60%! That's 60% more money, or 60% more bay restoration projects. You can check this with a home mortgage calculator. If you can afford, say, a $1,000 per month mortgage payment, you can get a 15-year mortgage of X dollars. But you can get a 30-year mortgage of 1.6 times. This means a 1.6x better home for the same amount of money.

So, the flush tax should, indeed, be emulated by other states, but they should make sure they can issue bonds for the full service lives of the project assets they are financing.

Chapter 3—Affordability

A year or so after the CWA was amended in 1987 to create the CWSRF, some folks at EPA began to wonder if people could afford the new loan program. Grants were free, but loans were not. Were communities across the country going to be able to repay these new loans?

So, they convened a meeting at EPA for the specific purpose of discussing the "concept of affordability." Most people there were EPA folks; but they invited a few outsiders. These discussions went very well, but there was one gentleman, an economist from EPA, who sat there with his arms folded across his chest, visibly upset. Finally, no longer able to contain himself, he blurted out: "In the world of classical economics, there is no such thing as the 'concept of affordability'." To which one of the outside participants gently responded: "Yes, but in the real world, there is no such thing as classical economics."

There are two affordability issues: community affordability and individual affordability. They are not mutually exclusive. You will have cases of individual *un*affordability in the wealthiest communities. And, perhaps surprisingly, there are also cases of individual *un*affordability in places where there is community *un*affordability as well.

We will deal with community *affordability* first.

Back in the mid-1990s, the Environmental Finance Center at the University of Maryland convened a meeting to discuss the dilemma of a small town in western Maryland situated on a tributary of the Potomac River. Just a few feet below the surface of the land was a stratum of solid bedrock. This was a rural community where all of the homes had septic systems. But because of the bedrock below, the septic systems did not work very well. The scientists from the state were puzzled with the readings they were getting on their downstream water quality tests. After much investigation, they concluded that the problem was coming from the little town's septic systems sitting on bedrock. So, the state ordered the town to install sewers. There were two problems with this requirement. First, to install the sewer mains they would have to blast out the bedrock. And, second, the homes in this town were not very close together. They were going to need several hundred extra feet of sewer mains. So, this was going to be a very expensive enterprise.

This was not a wealthy town and at the time, the average home value was well under $100,000. The residents, then, were understandably shocked when the engineers concluded that the project would cost $39,000 per home.

This is a classic case of where a grant is needed. It is a classic case of community *un*affordability.

Since 1997, community affordability has generally been measured by median household income (MHI). Remember that the "median" is not the "average." If there are three people living in a jurisdiction and they earn $10,000, $100,000, and $1 million respectively, then the "median income" is $100,000, the number in the middle. The average, on the other hand, is $370,000—quite a difference. So, using the "median" household income means that half of the people in the jurisdiction have greater incomes, and half have less. As you will read, it is those that have less that we must really be concerned about.

A very respected financial consulting firm, Raftelis Financial Consultants Inc. in Raleigh, North Carolina, has regularly conducted surveys in conjunction with the American Water Works Association (AWWA). In their most recent survey, Raftelis concluded that their respondents were paying 2.06% of MHI for both water and sewer services. This was up from 1.5% in 2010, an increase of about 30%—far more than the rate of inflation.

In 1997, EPA issued a document entitled "Combined Sewer Overflow Guidance for Financial Capability Assessment and Schedule Development." In this document, EPA set 2% of MHI as the threshold of how much a community can pay to comply with the CWA. If their sewer bills were over 2% of MHI, they could excuse themselves from some aspects of compliance based on their low income. If they were under 2%, the community had no defense; they had to comply. The 2.5% of MHI was later adopted by EPA to use for drinking water.

Note that Raftelis found that 2.06% of MHI was for both drinking water and wastewater.

So, community affordability has two distinct sides. There is the side that looks to communities like the poor little town in western Maryland. That's a classic *un*affordability question. They flat out can't pay for what they need to do. Then there are communities that aren't necessarily poor, but because of the exigencies of calculating the MHI (there are a lot of ratepayers just below the "median"), they fall under the 2% EPA threshold and must comply with the letter of the CWA. Sort of a "statistical affordability" problem.

The U.S. Conference of Mayors, the AWWA, the National Association of Clean Water Agencies (NACWA), and the Water Environment Federation

Chapter 3: Affordability

(WEF) have all been vocal in urging EPA to abandon the use of the MHI and, instead, look at other indices like the cost of living, mortgage and rental costs, as well as traditional income levels.

AWWA has been a national leader on the affordability question. Their most recent study, published in October 2017 focused primarily on individual affordability. Entitled "Addressing Affordability as a Necessary Element of Full-Cost Pricing," it was written by Tracy Mehan and Ian Gansler. Mehan is a former assistant administrator for Water at EPA, and Gansler is a Fulbright Scholar who was an intern at AWWA.

Their report referred to a 2016 EPA study "Drinking Water and Wastewater Utility Customer Assistance Programs." EPA's study reported on a survey that the Agency did of some 795 utilities. It found that 365 of them had some form of Customer Assistance Program (CAP). Unfortunately, EPA's survey found that nonprofit organizations were the most common funding source for CAPs. Society can't rely on nonprofit organizations to discharge its responsibility to the poor.

That said, regardless of how CAPs are funded, the first step is to identify those who can't pay their bills. There are several ways of doing this. The most straightforward is to tell customers that subsidies are available to households with less than $X annual income. Then ask those customers wishing subsidies to show their last one or two federal income tax returns. Another way is to contact the state agency handling food stamps and/or welfare payments. A third way is to find out which customers qualify for the federal Low-Income Household Energy Assistance Program (LIHEAP), which helps the poor pay their energy bills. (If there are confidentiality issues that prohibit obtaining the names of customers on food stamps, welfare, LIHEAP, etc. then the customers can again be asked to step forward voluntarily.)

Now, having identified those who cannot afford their utility service, we now need to address this individual affordability issue by identifying appropriate subsidies to help them pay their bills. Again, we can't rely on nonprofit organizations to do this forever.

There are at least three choices here.

First, the subsidy can come from general tax revenues, through some established state or local program. As you will see in our example below, we have identified 4,000 households (out of 100,000) who cannot afford their utility rates. They each need a subsidy of about $20 per month, or $240 per year, for a total of $480,000. In this first case, the subsidy would come from the state or local government, or both, out of their general revenues. In other words, the local or state government would take $480,000 out of their general fund and pay it to the utility.

Second, the subsidy can be a cross-subsidy. In this case, the ratepayers would be divided into two categories: (1) hardship; and (2) non-hardship. In this case, the subsidy for the hardship ratepayers comes from the non-hardship ratepayers. This method is illustrated below.

Finally, in the third case, the subsidy can come from all utility customers, whether or not they can be considered hardship customers.

Each of these options has advantages and disadvantages. The first option—subsidy from state or local tax revenues—may not be possible or feasible.

The difference between the last two options can be illustrated by a very simple example. This example considers only the case where there is no outside subsidy available to the utility—the program is funded by increasing some charges, or charges to some, or all, customers. The example is constructed for a medium-size community of 100,000 households. We will assume that the MHI for this community is about $50,000, which is about the national MHI. We will also assume that the MHI for our hardship cases is about $20,000, which is below the poverty level for a family of four.

Using an affordability number of 1% of MHI, the community in general should be paying about $500 a year, which would bring in about $50 million.

Our hardship cases should be paying only $200 per year. Assuming that 4% of the ratepayers are hardship cases, in order to provide them with a $300/year subsidy, we would need to generate about $1.2 million. That would mean a rate increase of only 2.4%. That's if everyone paid it, including the hardships. If not—if the hardships did not pay the extra 2.4%—then the other 96,000 customers would have to pay about $1 per month more to make up for them.

In either case, these are affordable numbers.

Chapter 4—Subsidies

Grants and subsidies are the same thing: they are gifts. A grant is generally a one-time event. Subsidies are generally ongoing, or at least pay for ongoing events. Subsidies have a long history in environmental finance.

When people think of subsidies, they usually think of helping the poor pay for things they can't afford. Right? Well, in the environmental infrastructure business, being poor has nothing to do with subsidies . . . most of the time.

There are four basic types of subsidies and two major distinctions. The types of subsidies are: (1) general; (2) supply-based; (3) targeted; or (4) demand-based. The distinctions are: (1) community; and (2) individual. Here are some examples.

First is the case of Loudoun County, Virginia—right outside of Washington, D.C. Currently, it is the richest county in the country. It has the highest MHI. Their median was $125,900 in 2017. That was the *median*. That means that 50% of the households earned *more than $125,900*.

In 2013, the Virginia CWSRF made a $7.3 million loan to Loudoun County at a subsidized rate of 1%. Why would anyone subsidize the richest county in America? If Virginia had made a 3% loan instead of a 1% loan, it would have saved $86,143 a year. It could have instead used this money to pay off bonds of $1.584 million for clean water projects for poor people in other places in Virginia, like Appalachia. Instead, Virginia gave a subsidized 1% loan to a county where over 180,000 people enjoy annual earnings of more than $125,000 a year.

The Loudoun County loan is an example of a general, supply-based subsidy to a community.

In one of my earlier books, I described a second type of subsidy. Borrowing characters from singer/songwriter John Cougar Mellencamp, I told a fanciful story about "Jack and Diane, doin' the best they can." They lived in a western state where there was a $300 statewide tax credit for installing a new clean-burning wood stove. This tax credit was as big a waste of money as the Loudoun County loan. Jack and Diane lived in a double-wide trailer in a valley in the mountains that was a "non-attainment area" for air quality purposes. The air was bad primarily because of all the old, dirty wood stoves that most people used. Jack and Diane didn't have much money. Diane worked as a cashier in a local grocery store. Jack did a lot of hunting and fishing and worked part time when he could find something to do. They had a big garden that they both tended. Between the produce from the garden and the fish and game that Jack got that was pretty much all they had. They had two kids, one of whom was asthmatic. Every time Jack and Diane lit their dirty old wood stove their little girl choked and gasped. They used the wood stove all year except summer. They had to. They had no other source of heat.

The state's $300 across the board tax credit did Jack and Diane no good at all. New, environmentally acceptable wood burning stoves cost about $3,500. There was no way Jack and Diane could go down to their local hardware store and drop their Visa card on the counter for a $3,500 wood stove even if the state gave them $300 back. They couldn't afford $3,500. They couldn't afford $3,200 either.

Jack and Diane's tax credit is an example of a general, supply-based subsidy for individuals.

Instead of this subsidy that everyone was eligible for, rich and poor alike, the state should have set up a 100% cash subsidy targeted only for people: (1) living in non-attainment areas; (2) below the poverty line; (3) with no other source of home heat; and (4) with a resident with a pulmonary ailment. If the state had done so, it would have been a targeted, demand-based subsidy for individuals. That would have been the right way to do things—save the state's money on those who didn't need it and get it to the people that do need it in meaningful and helpful amounts.

Another example was described in Chapter 3. It was the example about the poor community in western Maryland that needed sewers but was built on bedrock

This is a classic case of where a grant is needed. This is an example of a targeted, demand-based subsidy for a community.

So our four kinds of subsidies are:

1. General, Supply-Based Community Subsidies—the Loudoun County loan.

2. General, Supply-Based Individual Subsidies—Jack and Diane's state tax credit.

3. Targeted, Demand-Based Individual Subsidies—the way the state SHOULD have structured Jack and Diane's tax credit.

4. Targeted, Demand-Based Community Subsidies—the grant for the poor little town in Maryland with the septic tank problem.

Now the purpose of this chapter is twofold. First, to expose the wastefulness of general, supply-based subsidies; and, second, to tell you how targeted, demand-based subsidies can be put in place. So, the question should be: To what degree are the state's subsidies targeted to those households who can't afford to pay their water and sewer bills? The wisest policy is to find these poor folks, pay their bills, and save the rest of the money for more clean water projects in other parts of the state.

How do we find the poor folks who can't pay their water/sewer bills?

It is one thing to say that anyone with a water/sewer bill of more than 2% of their MHI gets a subsidy. It is another thing entirely to figure out who is eligible. Families don't get a note from the government each year informing them of their MHI. So, how do you know what their income level is? What surrogates can be used for estimating MHI and, hence, an appropriate subsidy? Some surrogates are participation in certain government programs, such as food stamps, that have financial eligibility criteria. Being on welfare is another financial criterion. Or being eligible for LIHEAP. This is a particularly effective targeted, demand-based individual subsidy program for those who need help paying their heating bills. Through the U.S. Department of Health and Human Services, the federal government delivered $3.39 billion of LIHEAP funds to states in 2017. No such program exists at this time for water or wastewater, but it certainly could in the future, especially as wastewater/stormwater costs continue to increase dramatically.

Finally, individual tax returns can be used to judge eligibility for subsidies. Utilities can tell their ratepayers to come forth—with their tax returns—if they would like a break on their water/sewer bills. Checking tax returns is probably the most accurate way to judge eligibility, but it is cumbersome. Elderly people with infirmities and those with medical problems won't come forward. In addition, the utility must hire staff to inspect the tax returns, which adds to their administrative cost.

The first thing the utility must do is figure out how much subsidy people will get.

The U.S. Department of Agriculture (USDA), in successfully managing its rural water and sanitation program since 1941, has also made it a policy to survey the water rates of surrounding communities when investigating affordability. When the USDA finds that a project is either not affordable per se, or that the project's annual debt service payments would put the utility's rates far in excess of those in neighboring districts, they then use a grant to buy down the cost of the project to affordable levels.

The USDA's grant (subsidy) policy is not perfect; but it far superior to the CWSRF programs where states indiscriminately give subsidies to rich and poor alike.[1] At least the USDA investigates the income levels and rates of its applicants and their neighboring districts and then targets its grants to those systems (not individuals) that actually need financial assistance in building their projects.

The next issue is for the utility to decide how much or how many subsidies they will provide.

For instance, if the full cost recovery tariff of a given utility results in a rate that is 2% of the MHI of its service area, a low-income person may be paying 5% or more of their income toward the water bill. Assuming that the local government and community members have decided on a maximum acceptable limit that a household should have to pay for water with respect to its percent of income, then the amount of the discount should equal the percentage difference between the maximum limit and the actual percent of household income that a low- income household would pay toward their water bill without the subsidy. For example, in the case where the full-cost recovery tariff is equal to 2% of household income of, let's say, $50,000, or $1,000 per year; this same $1,000 would equal 5% of the household income of one earning $20,000 per year. In such case, the system might charge (or give a rebate to) the $20,000 earner of $600 so that they, too, are paying 2% of their household income. The benefit to the utility of having discounts or lower rates for low-income customers is the increased likelihood of collecting payment from these customers; the subsidy makes it possible for these customers to pay more of their bills more regularly and promptly.

The important question that must be addressed once the amount of discount is determined, however, is who is going to pay for this discount? In order for the utility to continue to cover their costs of water delivery, they will have to charge all other customers' higher rates in order to make up the lost revenue from the low-income discount (subsidy). Some local governments are willing to pay for such subsidies from their tax collections as a form of social service for needy households. These are general, supply-based subsidies.

The same is true of national funds like LIHEAP. As noted above, today there is no LIHEAP-like program for water/sewer bills. But as noted above,

---

1. Some state CWSRF programs offer subsidies to all borrowers, but even deeper subsidies to communities with especially low MHIs.

Chapter 4: Subsidies

as utility rates continue to rise faster than MHI, the need for such a program will grow and should, at some point, catch the attention of the politicians.

As of this writing, another phenomenon is taking place that will militate for a national water fund. There are thousands of small community water systems in the United States, most of them built several generations ago. They all need upgrades, and these systems have no way to pay for them. The customers can't afford it. There are no good jobs in these small towns. People are moving away. This situation cries out for a national water fund. Again, someday the politicians may get it.

Here is a final anti-climactic note about being careful about "perverse incentives." A "perverse incentive" is when water is sold to low-income customers without any volume restrictions. In such cases, it has been observed that some poor people paying a nominal amount for their water will actually sell it to other customers who are paying regular rates. This doesn't happen too often in the United States. But it does happen in some countries.

There are stories of intrepid entrepreneurs in Haiti who somehow get access to a tank truck, go into the rich neighborhoods in the middle of the night, open the fire hydrants and fill up their trucks (there are no fire hydrants in poor areas), chlorinate it, drive it back to the poor areas and sell it. In this case, the folks they sell it too have no public water supply. They have to rely on bottled water, which is very expensive. So, the entrepreneurs in Haiti are really performing a valuable social service.

Chapter 5—Tariffs

The two preceding chapters dealt with affordability and subsidies. Both of these concepts play out in the rates, or tariffs, that utilities charge their customers.

Efficient tariffs reduce the cost of providing environmental utility services to customers. As the cost of maintaining environmental quality continues to rise, it will be important to keep rates for existing services as low as possible. This chapter will discuss the various types of tariffs and how they can help achieve the goal of lower cost services.

Characteristics of Good Tariffs

The following are some of the key characteristics of well-considered tariffs for water and wastewater systems:

- Revenue Sufficiency/Cost Recovery: tariffs produce revenue that is equal to the real cost of supplying the water or wastewater services.

- Fairness: equals must be treated equally—in other words, the prices charged to customers are equal to the costs imposed on the system by those customers.

- Resource Conservation: pricing decisions should not promote the unwise use of water resources.

- Net Revenue Stability: prices should allow the utility to have sufficient income to meet its operating costs, even when quantities demanded are below a normal level.

- Transparency: pricing structures should be able to be understood by every consumer.

- Ease of Implementation: the pricing structure should not impose significant administrative costs on the utility.

- Affordability: the prices charged to customers should be within a standard limit of affordability.

There are two basic types of tariffs: those that have a fixed charge and those that have a volumetric charge.

A fixed charge is one where the amount of money charged to a customer is the same each month and is independent of the amount of water that customer consumes.

In places where there are no water meters, volumetric charges are not a viable option because there is no way to accurately measure how much water each customer consumes. In this situation, a *single-part tariff or fixed charge tariff* using equal monthly charges is the only available option.

When setting the fixed charge, or fee, for all customers, the utility must first determine its own costs for delivering the amount of water demanded by all customers because the total revenue that the utility will receive must cover the utility's total costs plus provide funds for maintenance and repairs. A utility may define different "classes" of customers, so that residential customers are charged different (usually less) fixed rates than business customers since businesses tend to consume more water than residential users.

Fixed charges, when used alone, have two major drawbacks. Firstly, consumers are given no incentive to economize on water use since each additional gallon of water comes free of charge. Secondly, as water use increases, as will certainly happen with a growing population and a developing economy, the utility's ability to recover its costs by the fixed charge will diminish as the costs of meeting growing needs increases.

The other type of tariff has volumetric pricing.

A utility that has water meters on all or most household connections is able to monitor the amount of water that each customer uses and is thus able to charge according to the amount of water consumed each month. When setting this price, the utility should attempt to set the volumetric charge at the cost per unit of water provided to each consumer.

To calculate the total charge for each customer group, utilities multiply the amount of water consumed by the price per cubic foot of water. This produces a uniform volumetric tariff structure where the price per unit of water is the same regardless of how much water is purchased in total by each customer.

In this example, a uniform volumetric charge is used where each consumer group is charged the same volumetric price; the next section discusses other forms of volumetric charges.

There are a small number of accepted methods for designing volumetric charges that must be considered when setting tariffs, so that the utility is able to select a tariff that will achieve full recovery of the costs to deliver water service, while trying to achieve the other goals of equity, affordability, and economic efficiency. The four volumetric pricing design options, in addition to the uniform volumetric charge that was described above, are: (1) increasing block tariff (IBT); (2) declining block tariff (DBT); (3) seasonal pricing; and (4) zonal pricing.

Increasing Block Tariff

In theory, IBT can achieve three objectives simultaneously:

1. Promote affordability by providing the poor with affordable access to a "subsistence block" of water.
2. Achieve efficiency by confronting consumers in the highest price block with the real cost of the water they are using.
3. Raise sufficient revenues to recover costs.

In practice, however, IBTs often fail to meet any of the three objectives mentioned above, in part because they tend to be poorly designed. Many IBTs fail to reach cost recovery and economic efficiency objectives, usually because the upper consumption blocks are not priced at sufficiently high levels and/or because the first subsidized block is so large that almost all residential consumers never consume beyond this level.

When used in a multipart tariff, the increasing block pricing scheme affects only the volumetric part of the total tariff; the fixed charge remains the same over all the customer groups. Calculating the total charge for each customer group using an IBT first requires delineating the number of blocks and the quantity of water allowed in each block. Customers will pay the fixed charge plus the sum of the products of the amount of water consumed in each block multiplied by the per unit price of water in each block.

The next tariff design option to be discussed is the DBT.

Declining Block Tariff

A DBT is the opposite of an IBT. With a DBT, consumers face a high volumetric charge up to the specified quantity of the first block. Then any water consumed beyond this level, and up to the next block, is charged at a lower rate, and so on for as many blocks as the tariff utilizes.

The DBT structure was designed to reflect the fact that when raw water supplies are abundant, large industrial customers often impose lower average costs because they enable the utility to capture economies of scale in water source development, transmission, and treatment. This tariff design has gradually fallen out of favor, in part because marginal costs, properly defined, are now relatively high in many parts of the world, and there is thus increased interest in promoting water conservation by the largest customers. The DBT structure is also often politically unattractive because it results in high volume users paying lower average water prices.

Seasonal Pricing

The third type of volumetric tariff is the seasonal charge.

In some circumstances the marginal cost of supplying water to customers may vary by seasons. In such cases, water tariffs can be used to signal customers that the costs of water supply are not constant across the seasons. Summer water use tends to be much higher for households that have gardens and any other high water uses; the increase in water use is usually found to be in outdoor water use, while indoor water use tends to remain constant throughout the year.

When the cost to provide water services changes according to the seasons, then utilities can charge higher prices during the more costly seasons (usually summer) and lower prices during the less expensive seasons (usually winter).

Zonal Pricing

The last type of volumetric tariff is zonal pricing.

Zonal pricing can occur when the marginal cost to provide water service varies according to the location of the customer. In this case, utilities can charge higher volumetric rates to the customers that live in an area that is more costly to serve, and lower volumetric rates to those who live in areas that are cheaper to serve.

It may cost the water utility more to deliver water to outlying communities due, for example, to higher elevations and increased pumping costs. Zonal prices can be used to ensure that users receive the economic signal that living in such areas involves substantially higher water supply costs. Nevertheless, this type of special tariff is only appropriate if the costs to serve the area are significantly higher than for the rest of the community.

The goals of full cost recovery and economic efficiency are achieved when utilities charge customers according to the cost that each customer imposes on the system. If the cost to deliver water is the same for all of the utility's customers, then a uniform volumetric charge that is set equal to the cost of water delivery is the most efficient. The DBT is used when the cost to deliver large amounts of water is cheaper than for small amounts of water. When the marginal cost of water is high, IBT is usually chosen over a DBT since it charges higher rates to customers that demand higher levels of water.

Chapter 6—Financing Environmental Projects

As we have said before, we will have to pay more to maintain our quality of life. So, it behooves us to produce environmental services as inexpensively as possible.

The lowest cost for environmental improvement projects results from financing them over the longest possible term. The longest possible term depends directly on the service life of the assets being financed.

The easiest part of this equation is to discuss service life.

Every capital asset, especially equipment, has a term of years over which it can typically be used. Good home washers and dryers last 10 years. Automobiles, 5-10 years. Most people don't finance their washers and dryers. But a lot of people pay for their cars over time. Payment terms of 5-6 years are very common, and occasionally 7-10 years.

There is an enormous difference between decisions to buy or finance personal items such as cars and washers and dryers versus financing major capital assets used by public agencies.

The best example of this involves a school board buying a school bus. School buses last 10 years. So if the school board issues a 10-year bond to pay for it that is completely appropriate. On the other hand, if they issue a five-year bond, their taxpayers for the next five years will be paying much more than they should, and those who move into the school districts and begin paying school taxes in year six will get a free ride (so to speak) for five years.

The opposite side of this coin is the school district that issues a 20-year bond. That is just lunacy. The taxpayers in years 11-20 will be paying for nothing.

Contrast the school board's decision with that of a 50-year-old homebuyer who has to choose between a 15- and a 30-year mortgage. The service life of the house will certainly be at least 30 years. So, why not a 30-year mortgage? Well, this particular homebuyer plans to retire at age 65. He really doesn't know what his financial condition will be at that time, and he doesn't want to guess. In short, he doesn't want to be paying the mortgage for more than the next 15 years. So, although the monthly payment on a 15-year mortgage is significantly more expensive than the monthly payment on a 30-year mortgage, the homebuyer is making a very prudent personal financial decision. Contrast this with the school board members looking at a new school bus with a 10-year service life. Financing it for any term less than 10 years is imprudent and financing it for more than 10 years is crazy.

So, in personal finance, term is justifiably a personal decision. But in public finance, paying for equipment over the full term of its service life is the most prudent course of action.

You may have wondered about the term of public finance loans for land. The service life of land is infinite (at least most of the time). Well, in the public finance market there are 100-year bonds. For assets with exceedingly long service lives, like land or sewer mains, the finance markets dictate the term of municipal bonds to finance them. As of now, 100 years is about as long as the markets can stomach.

As noted above, the term of a loan has an enormous impact on annual debt service payments.

To put the concept of the power of term into full perspective, below is a table that sets forth the first year's annual payments on a $100 loan at an interest rate of 5%:

Term	Payment
1 year	$105
2 years	$55
3 years	$38
4 years	$30
5 years	$25
10 years	$15
20 years	$10
30 years	$8
40 years	$7.50

As you can see, term has a hugely significant impact on annual debt service payments.

We need to mention that there are two general ways that loans are repaid. The first is called the level principal payment (LPP) method. This is exactly what it says. If you have a five-year loan, in each of the five years you pay off one-fifth of the principal. If you have a 20-year loan, in each year you pay off 1/20th of the principal, and so on. These payments decline over time because

Chapter 6: Financing Environmental Projects

the interest you are paying is charged only on the outstanding balance that is declining.

The second way to repay loans is by the level payment (LP) method. This is also exactly what it says. The payment is the same every year. The mechanism at work here is that as loan principal is paid off, instead of the annual payment declining (as is the case with an LPP loan), the next year's payment contains more principal to make up for the lower interest and to keep the payments level. So the first year's payment is almost all interest and the last year's payment is almost all principal.

Below is a table that sets forth the first year's annual payments on a $100 LP loan at an interest rate of 5%:

Term	Payment
1 year	$105
2 years	$54
3 years	$37
4 years	$28
5 years	$23
10 years	$13
20 years	$8
30 years	$7
40 years	$6

Unfortunately, the formula for calculating the annual payment on an LP loan involves a complicated equation. There's no point in going into algebra in this book. Suffice it to say that a good financial calculator or tables in a mortgage book will get you where you need to go.

Note that with the LP method, the annual payment is always the same. So if you take out a 30-year loan in 2018, your payment in 2019 will be the same as your payment in 2047. This is a good thing. As you know, the value of money declines over time. An old friend of mine took out a 30-year mortgage many, many years ago. The day she took it out, the payment was $131 a month and her annual salary was $6,000. Thirty years later, her last monthly payment was also $131, but by then her annual salary was over $120,000. So, as a percentage of her salary, the LP loan declined over time. The same is true in public finance. The last annual payment on a 30-year LP loan will definitely be a much smaller percentage of the agency's budget than the first payment.

So, the lesson here is to finance public assets over the longest possible term, which will be directly dictated by their service lives. Then you will know that you are using the most inexpensive means of "paying for tomorrow."

Chapter 7—Credit Enhancement

The words "credit enhancement" don't usually apply to individual people. Oh, when you are young and your parents sign your first mortgage, they are guarantying payment to your mortgage lender. The same is true if they sign on your auto loan. These guaranties, although casual, are a form of credit enhancement. Parents and rich uncles and aunts are the usual form of personal credit enhancement. But sometimes when you are making a commercial purchase and paying for it over time, the vendor will want you to get a letter of credit (LoC) from your bank to guaranty your payment. Again, this is credit enhancement at the personal level. No one, however, calls these personal guaranties "credit enhancement." Those words apply to institutions and institutional debt.

From time to time, governments, businesses, and institutions have trouble paying their bills. When they default or are delinquent with debt payments, their credit ratings suffer. Sometimes the problems are transient and can be readily solved. In the late 1970s, the city of New York went bankrupt. Recently, the city of Detroit did the same. Both, however, pulled themselves out of financial trouble.

So, what is "credit enhancement"? Essentially, "credit enhancement" is a euphemism for reducing the risk of non-payment on debt. In general, credit enhancement is used on (non-federal) government debt as well as some major corporate and institutional debt.

If lenders or investors believe there is a high risk of loss, they will demand high interest rates to compensate for the risk. They will also offer only short terms to minimize the time in which something can go wrong. Reducing the risk of default on public debt results in longer terms and lower interest rates. Longer terms and lower rates mean lower annual payments. Lower annual payments mean that more projects get done, and the ones that are done have a greater chance of success.

Take the case of a bus rapid transport (BRT) project in a major international city. (BRT projects are considered climate change projects because they can significantly reduce the pollution caused by automobile traffic.) The money to repay debt issued to finance the project can only come from two sources: fares and subsidies from the city. If the annual debt service payments (ADSPs) are high then the fares must be high or the subsidies must be high, or both. High fares mean lower ridership, which is like shooting yourself in the foot since getting people out of automobiles and on to BRTs is how you reduce GHG emissions and retard climate change. That is the point of BRT projects. By the same token, higher BRT subsidies mean that some other vital area of government, like public health, or education, or housing, or food, is getting less money. High interest rates and short terms spell a lose/lose situation for climate change projects like BRTs.

So the purpose of credit enhancement is to reduce the risk of default or delinquency on debt. And the goal of using credit enhancement is to drive down the ADSP, or cost, on project debt.

There are eight major strategies for enhancing credit or driving down the cost, or ADSP, of project debt. All of these strategies involve removing—or at least making very remote—the risk of financial loss. As we have said, short terms and high interest rates can doom many environmental infrastructure projects. It should be noted, however, that although all of these strategies are widely used, some of them are used much more internationally than they are in the United States. In addition, many of the strategies such as "second loss reserves" are used in financing infrastructure projects with much higher risk profiles—like urban mass transit or toll roads. That said, it should also be noted that in the future—as the business of delivering water and wastewater services evolves—these public utilities will be asked to finance projects that are not directly supported by rate bases. In such cases, they may well need credit enhancement.

Here are the eight strategies for enhancing the credit rating of debt by reducing the risk of loss.

Strategy #1: Lock Boxes

"Lock boxes" are the easiest form of credit enhancement to employ. The phrase "lock box" is just a short form way of saying "revenue segregation." If a public utility sends out its own bills and receives payments from its customers, they should stop doing this. Instead they should have the payments made directly to a major bank that will collect the money in a special trust account. That account should be structured such that the bank is required to hold all funds in that account until there is enough to make the annual payment on the utility's debt. The bank would make the payment on the utility's behalf and pay any remaining funds over into the utility's operating account.

Chapter 7: Credit Enhancement

This procedure assures lenders, creditors, and bondholders that the first dollars collected will go to them. The bank will not transfer funds into the utility's operating account (or any other account) until *all* of the money is there to pay your debts that year.

Lender/creditors like lock boxes because they minimize the possibility that there won't be enough funds to pay then. They also minimize the possibility that any of the money will be diverted to other uses instead of paying them.

Strategy #2: Liens

The reason that water/wastewater system debt is so highly regarded is because ratepayers religiously pay their water/sewer bills. The same is pretty much true with electricity bills and even bills for other electronic services. When one of these types of utilities needs to make capital improvement to its system, it borrows the money it needs and adds the annual payments to the rates that its customers pay.

Now take the case where your local government is concerned about defective septic systems. Or, as part of their stormwater strategy, they want homeowners to replace the asphalt on their driveways with porous, or permeable, pavement. Or, they want homes along waterways to be raised up on stilts (pillars) to protect them against extreme weather events. And, the local government wants one of its agencies to administer these programs. Now what? Is someone who is forced to replace his septic system going to repay the debt for this with the same religious zeal that normal water-sewer-electric power ratepayers pay their bills. The point is who knows?

The answer to this dilemma is liens. Put a lien on the property. Then, if the homeowner doesn't pay his debt to you, you can legally move against his property. This is especially important with small commercial borrowers. The strip shopping center that replaces the asphalt in their parking lot with permeable pavement, just might not make its payment next year. In that case, the local government can move against the shopping center itself to recover the missing funds. This is much safer than an unsecured loan to the owner.

In some cases, a state statute or a local ordinance will be needed to authorize these kinds of liens. But this concept has a very silver lining.

Take the case of a homeowner who wants to spend $15,000 to replace his driveway with permeable pavement. Under normal circumstances, he would go to his bank and get a second mortgage loan. In such case, his bank might give him a seven-year loan at 7% interest. The homeowner's monthly payment on this second mortgage loan would be $226.39.

Now, the pavement will last 30+ years. So, the local government's finance program could offer the homeowner a 30-year loan at its cost of funds, which today should be about 3.5%. In such case, the homeowner's monthly payment would be $67.96. So, think about it. How many more people would install permeable pavement if it only cost $68 a month versus $226 a month. That's the point of programs like these: the lower the cost, the more projects get done, the greater the environmental benefit.

Strategy #3: Tranching

Tranche is a French word meaning "slice." The concept here is to slice a debt into pieces with ascending order of risk of loss. This may sound complicated; but it really isn't.

Let's say you owe six people $100 each. Who gets paid first? What if you only have $500 to make the payments with? Which of your creditors isn't going to get his $100?

Here's what needs to be done. (Again, it sounds complicated, but good lawyers can handle it in a heartbeat.)

In advance (and this must be done in advance), you line your creditors up from A through F. You tell A he will get paid first. You tell B he will get paid second. C, third. And so on. So, if you only have $500 to pay off $600 of debts, you know who doesn't get paid. It is F. You should also know that A will only expect, say, about a 3% interest rate on his loan. Whereas F— because of the high risk of non-payment that he's taking—will expect considerably more. He may expect 15-20%. This is why tranching is important. The tranches should not all be the same amount. F's tranche should be the smallest. Let's say you borrowed $300 from A, lesser amounts from B-E, and only borrow $10 from F. At a 20% interest rate you would have to pay F $2 interest. You can afford it.

Here is a more realistic example of tranching.

Let's say there are 1,000 apartment units in various suitable places. Now, the probability that *all* 1,000 tenants will make full and timely rental payments in any given month is close to zero. Out of 1,000 tenants, at least a few will be sick, dead, broke, forgetful, or gone. Conversely, however, the probability that all 1,000 tenants will default on their payment is also close to zero.

What is the probability that one tenant will not make his payment? It is very high; close to 100%. What is the probability that five tenants will miss their payments? Again, it is very high; close to 100%.

Chapter 7: Credit Enhancement

What is the probability that 100 tenants—that's 10% of the total—will miss their monthly rental payment? It is very low; very low, indeed.

Now, let's say that you want to buy these apartments—all of them. The current owner will sell them—all of them—for $70 million. Let's say that the monthly rent for each apartment is $600 and maintenance, taxes, and insurance are $1.2 million a year, or $100 per month per apartment.

Now, here's a new wrinkle. You are going to have all of the tenants pay their rent directly to a "lock box" at a Trustee Bank. You will instruct the Trustee Bank to take $100 out of every tenant's monthly payment and put it in an operating account for taxes, maintenance, and insurance. You then instruct Trustee Bank to put the balance, $500 per tenant per month, into an escrow account. That means that if every tenant paid his rent in full, you would have $500,000 a month in rental income in your escrow account. That is a total of $6 million a year.

Now, you want to finance the purchase of the buildings. So, you go to the bank and tell them that you can pay $500,000 a month. You'd like a 20-year mortgage and you've heard that the going interest rate is 6%. So, you ask for a $70 million mortgage.[1]

What do you think the banker will say?

I think the banker would ask you a politely rhetorical question, something like: "And, how much of a down payment are you planning on making?" Of course, if the buildings cost $70 million and you asked for a $70 million mortgage, you obviously didn't plan on making *any* down payment. If the banker had agreed, you would have scored an infinite leverage deal. You would have bought the buildings entirely with OPM—"other peoples' money." This doesn't happen . . . at least with banks.

Bankers like down payments. They like to know that their borrowers have their own skin in the game. One of the major reasons for this is, as we know, the possibility that all $500,000 will materialize, in other words, that all 1,000 tenants will pay promptly each month—is zero. The banker knows this too. So, he is not going to give you $70 million.

Now, let's say that you take the same deal to a smart investment banker. The investment banker will know, as we said above that the probability that 100 tenants, or 10%, won't pay their rent is very, very small. So, he issues a new instruction to the Trustee Bank: *put the first 900 tenant payments into a new account called "Escrow A."* Since the probability that at least 900 out of 1,000 tenants will pay is virtually 100%, the investment banker knows he

---

[1] A $70 million debt for 20 years at a rate of 6% requires a monthly payment of $500,000.

can get a good interest rate on these bonds. He can get a 5% interest rate. In addition, in the bond market he knows he can get a 25-year term.

So, instead of one bond, he has two; or more correctly, he has one bond with two tranches. There is the "A Tranche" of 90% of the purchase price, or $63 million. The annual payment on this A Tranche is $4.47 million.

Now, what about the other $7 million?

Well, now the investment banker creates another tranche, this time called the "Z Tranche."[2] The Z Tranche is $7 million. But because it carries virtually all of the risk of loss, it requires a shorter term and a much higher interest rate.

So, the Z Tranche will have a 20-year term and will carry an interest rate of 15%. It will also be an LPP bond.

Remember Trustee Bank is putting $6 million a year into escrow accounts, of which $4.5 million is going into the Escrow A account. Please note that after making the payment on the A Tranche, there will be $30,000 left in this account, which is your profit.

Next, the investment banker will also instruct Trustee Bank to put the other $1.5 million of rental income into a second new escrow account, the Escrow Z account.

Now, the first year's annual payment on Z Tranche includes 15% interest on $7 million or $1.05 million plus the level annual principal payment of 1/20th of $7 million, or about $350,000 for a total payment of $1.4 million. So, your profit in year one on this $70 million transaction is $30,000 from the A Tranche and $100,000 from the Z Tranche. But your ROI is infinite since you didn't invest a penny of your own money! You bought $70 million worth of buildings entirely with OPM. Congratulations!

But, from day one on, it gets even better. You are paying your mortgage by the LPP method. So your payment declines each year and your profit increases by the same amount. The only problem with the Z Tranche is that it is very expensive, so it must be minimized.

Let's look at another example from another environmental medium.

Instead of 1,000 rental apartment units, think of 100 climate change projects, each costing $100 million, for a total of $10 billion, and originating in 100 different countries none of which is in default on any of its foreign loans. Now, investors might believe that at least 90 of these loans are completely secure: absent a global economic meltdown, they will never default. But, they might feel that between 0 and 10 of these projects might get in trouble.

---

2. By convention, investment bankers refer to the tranche that carries the lion's share of the risk of loss the "Z Tranche." The Z Tranche is an equity tranche.

Chapter 7: Credit Enhancement

So, one might be tempted to break these projects into two tranches with A Tranche funded by inexpensive, long-term debt and Z Tranche funded by costly equity.

Below an example of the cost of debt and equity with a debt/equity mix of 90:10. The debt is for a 20-year term at a 5% rate. The ROI for the equity is 25%.

	Equity Tranche (25%)	Debt Tranche (5%)	Total
Investment	$100	$900	$1,000
Annual Payment Required	$25	$72.22	$97.22

You can tell intuitively that something is wrong here. The equity eats up almost 25% of the annual payment but provides only 10% of the needed cash, whereas the debt furnishes 90% of the cash for only about 75% of the annual payment.

Remembering that our goal in environmental finance is to bring the greatest benefit to the largest number of people at the lowest possible cost, we need to find a way to get rid of the equity component. We must replace the equity. This leads us right into Strategy #4.

Enter a concept we will call a self-funded reserve (SFR).

Strategy #4: Self-Funded Reserves

Municipal revenue bonds in the United States are often structured with SFRs. Here, the borrower puts up a reserve against its own default. In the United States, this is done singly. This means that if a water system issues a bond, they generally add to the principal one full year's debt service and place it into the hands of a bank trustee. This is to protect against transient problems. A major water main break is a good example. Here the problem might be so severe and so acute that it eats up all of the utility's cash reserves and the money it had put aside for its next annual debt service payment. In such case, when the Trustee Bank does not receive the system's payment on the due date, it dips into the reserve fund that had been set up. Theoretically, once the system gets its repairs done and puts its fiscal house back in order, it should replace the reserve funds that had been spent.

On the international scene, SFRs are very different. The mechanism I just described in the United States works for one project and one bond. But on the international stage, it would work at the fund level, i.e., a fund composed of 100 or more projects.

Here each project would contribute 10% to a reserve fund; but, in this case, it would be a "common" reserve fund. In the U.S. example, the reserve protected against the borrower's own delinquency. In this new climate change example, *each borrower's reserve fund protects against the defaults of each and every one of the projects in the fund.* So, in our example, each of the 100 projects would contribute to a common SFR. Please note that common SFRs are largely unnecessary in financing traditional water/wastewater projects, but they will certainly come into play as organizations are called upon to finance more exotic ones.

An SFR is, essentially, an over-borrowing that is placed into an escrow account to pay for defaults. Thus, if a project cost is $1,000, the borrower acquires $1,100 and puts the additional $100 into an escrow account. The SFR is fully amortized by the annual payments of the borrower. This raises the cost to the borrower but not nearly so much as does equity. (Internationally, private equity plays a much larger role in public finance than it does in the United States.) If a borrower acquires $1,100 and puts the $100 into an escrow account—instead of using 10% equity—his annual payment would increase to $88.27,[3] but far less than the combined $97.22 cost of the $900 debt and $100 equity in the example in the above section.

There are two additional benefits to SFRs. SFRs provide debt investors additional protection against loss *over time*. SFRs are invested in interest-bearing accounts. They grow. Furthermore, as each loan repayment is made by the borrower, the outstanding balance on the debt declines. The combined effect of a growing reserve and a shrinking debt balance is a significant reduction in the investors' risk of loss over time.

Finally, there are some political benefits in the SFR concept as well. If the 100 developing countries borrow an extra $1 billion on top of the $10 billion they need for their projects, and they default, then the money they lose is their own. There is a certain fundamental principal of justice here: if you ask for help, you must first be willing to help yourself. All investors feel more comfortable if a project sponsor (borrower) has its own skin in the game. The SFR is just that: the borrower's own skin in the game.

So, Strategy #4 is: replace equity with SFRs wherever possible.

---

3. This amount was calculated by using the same 20-year term and 5% interest rate as in the above example.

Strategy #5: Tax Revenue Intercepts

Think unrelated tax receipts!

Tax revenue intercepts (TRIs) are credit support mechanisms that can be used to assuage investors' fears of non-payment of local government debt. It is important to note that these mechanisms do not replace usual income streams. They are not the source of repayments. Rather these mechanisms are stand-bys, fallbacks, or safety nets, just in case revenues are off or the subsidies aren't enough. They serve as guaranties. Here are some examples.

In the late 1970s, the city of New York was bankrupt. Nevertheless, they needed to borrow money to undertake needed civic infrastructure projects. But no one would lend to them. At that time there was a sales tax in New York State that was shared with local governments. The tax was 5% in those days, 3% of which went to the state and 2% of which went to the city. The city collected all of the taxes incurred in the city and forwarded the state's share to the state treasurer.

To overcome the city's credit problem, the city and state enacted laws to provide that all sales tax revenues in the city would be paid into an account in the city's name at an international bank acting as a trustee (a "lock box"). So, the city, itself, never legally touched this money. The bank forwarded the state's share to the state treasurer. But the bank held the city's share for the benefit of its lenders. (As the city dutifully made each payment on its debt, the bank trustee would release the funds it then held into the city's general account.) And so, the city was then able to borrow money by pledging the hundreds of millions of dollars of its sales tax revenues—in the hands of an independent bank fiduciary—to its new lenders. So, the city's local sales tax revenues were "intercepted" for the benefit of its creditors. Note also that the intercepted revenues had nothing at all to do with any projects. They were unrelated tax receipts.

India has an even more powerful variation of the local tax intercept. This mechanism has been successfully used to support local water system debt in the state of Tamil Nadu. Here, certain tax revenues are *owned by the local governments*, but they are *collected by the state governments*. In this case, the local government and the state government entered into an agreement with the local government's lenders such that if the local government ever failed to make a timely loan repayment, the lender could go to the state which would "intercept" enough of the local government's tax revenues to make up the missed payment to the lender. A similar tax revenue sharing structure exists in Turkey.

In Mexico, certain tax revenues are legally shared by the federal and state governments. Because both the federal and state governments participate in the benefits of these monies, they are called "participaciones." These *participaciones* are collected by the federal government. If a state borrows money, it, of course, promises to repay the money with interest from its general revenues. But in addition, the state may pledge that in the event that it fails to pay in the normal course of business, the lender may apply to the federal government, which is legally obligated to "intercept" the state's *participacion* of the tax and pay the state's lenders whatever they are owed. Standard & Poor's (S&P) reported that in 2009, 80% of all municipal bonds issued in Mexico were supported by *participacion* agreements.

There is another variation of tax intercept that might be called a "super tax intercept"—"super" in the sense of "above." Recall in the above city of New York example, the state of New York also owned 3% out of the 5% sales tax revenue. This money belonged to the state, not the city. Nevertheless, if the state really wanted to assist the city, and the state did not want to issue its own guaranty (or was itself not creditworthy enough to issue a guaranty as in the case of Argentina), then the state could have agreed that its share of the sales tax revenue could have been pledged to the repayment of the city's debt.

As noted above, these credit support mechanisms are not the source of debt repayment; rather they are a stand-by or a fallback in case the borrower cannot make a debt payment. But they are exceedingly powerful. They ease investors' fears of non-payment to the point where they will accept lower interest rates and significantly longer terms on their investments.

TRIs are widely used abroad. But they started in the United States in the 1980s with school district debt where a given state had enacted a student per capita aid formula. In such case, if a school district defaulted on its bond issue, the bondholders could go to the state treasurer who would be legally required to "intercept" the per capita aid payment to the school district, and pay it to the bondholders (as much as they were owed) instead. TRIs can provide powerful support to debt, helping to reduce interest rates and lengthen terms.

Strategy #6: Externally Funded Guaranties

Strategy #6 involves guaranties that are funded with cash; but unlike the case with SFRs, the cash comes from another source, generally a government program that funded it.

Chapter 7: Credit Enhancement

At $125+ billion, the CWSRF is the largest dedicated environmental finance program in the world. It is an externally funded source of guaranties.

All 50 states and the commonwealth of Puerto Rico participate in the CWSRF program, which are managed at the state level. Since its inception in 1987, Congress has funded the CWSRF at various levels. These funds are appropriated to EPA and then distributed to the states under a congressionally approved formula. Under the CWA, in order to receive CWSRF funds, each state must appropriate $1 for every $5 it receives from EPA.

Today the "size" of the CWSRF is $125+ billion, which means that $125+ billion of projects have been funded. The "net assets" of the CWSRF are $40+ billion. "Net assets" equals: (1) the congressionally contributed funding; plus (2) the 1:5 matching funds appropriated by the states; and (3) interest earned on funds that have been loaned. The difference between the program "size" ($100+ billion) and its "net assets" is called "leverage." The CWSRF's leverage ratio is only about 2:1.

S&P has studied the default histories of municipal bonds for almost a century. The default history on bonds issued to fund public wastewater projects is approximately 0.04, or 2500:1. In January 2011, S&P published a document requesting comment on, inter alia, a new total leverage ratio for anyone guarantying public wastewater project debt. S&P said that if the guarantor wanted to maintain its highest investment grade credit rating (AAA), the maximum leverage ratio could be no higher than 75:1.

With $40+ billion of net assets, at a 75:1 leverage ratio, the CWSRF has the potential to leverage $3 trillion.

Why is the CWSRF important to a discussion of credit enhancement? Specifically because the 51 CWSRFs have the legal authority to issue guaranties. And, theoretically, their collective guaranties, up to a total of $3 trillion would be rated AAA.

Now, what is most important to realize is that the guaranties offered by CWSRFs are not government guaranties in the legal sense. No, when a CWSRF issues a guaranty, the underlying documents specifically provide that the only source of the guaranty is the CWSRF's net assets. In other words, these CWSRF guaranties are not the legal promise of any government; rather they are guaranties backed by enormous amounts of cash.

When you think of "externally funded guaranties" like these, think of a bank LoC. What is the bank's LoC backed with? It is backed with the bank's equity; its own funds. Here in our example, the CWSRF guaranties are backed by each CWSRF's net assets. No legal promises; just cash.

Strategy #7: Legal Guaranties

A legal guaranty is an enforceable contract whereby one party promises to make full payment for the debt of a second party if the second party fails to make a full and timely payment on such debt. If you lend $1,000 to your neighbor, and the neighbor's rich uncle guaranties the debt in writing, and if your neighbor fails to make an agreed-upon payment at an agreed-upon time, you can take your written guaranty from the rich uncle into court and compel him to pay.

The point here to consider is that the value of any guaranty is directly related to the strength of the guarantor's credit. If, for example, the U.S. government guarantees one of your debts, you would be rewarded with the longest term and the lowest interest rate in the market. If, on the other hand, you decided to guaranty a U.S. Treasury bond, it wouldn't mean squat, other than being the funniest thing the bankers had seen in years.

So, a good lawyer will make sure the guaranty works, and the strength of the guarantor's credit will give it value.

Strategy #8: Financial Guaranty Insurance

Strategy #8 is to use financial guaranty insurance, which, in the United States, is generally called municipal bond insurance, to enhance your credit.

Before the subprime mortgage crisis in 2008, there were 15 municipal bond insurance companies, which, in 2005, guaranteed almost 60% of the roughly $400 billion of municipal bonds issued that year. In 2011, there was one company. Now there are four. Competition turned these companies from guarantying good, old-fashioned, low-risk municipal bonds into guarantors of wild, exotic financial instruments that were tied to home mortgages. The entire industry got burned by defaults in these subprime mortgages.

So, should financial guaranty insurance be used to enhance the credit of a particular transaction? The answer is: if it works, yes. What does this mean? It means that if the bond insurance will lower your interest rate more than enough to cover the cost of the insurance premium, then you should use it.

Because of the checkered history of bond insurers, their insured bonds sometimes do not trade as well as an uninsured bond with the same rating. In other words, if city A, with a AA credit rating issues a bond, and city B, with only a BBB rating but which buys insurance from a AA-rated insurer, issues an identical bond, you will often see city A's bond trading an a better interest rate than city B's.

Chapter 7: Credit Enhancement

So, the appropriate way to deal with bond insurance is to determine at what rate the two bond insurers bonds are trading. Then determine where your bonds would trade without insurance. Then request a quote from the two insurers. Then determine if the lower payments because of the higher credit rating will more than offset the cost of the insurance.

In general, the rule is that the insurance premium should eat up just under half of the spread between what your bonds would trade at with the insurance versus without the insurance. In other words, if your bonds would sell at 5% without the insurance and 4.5% with the insurance, then the premium should cost you about 0.2%, which means your all-in rate with the insurance would be 4.7%. So you would save the difference between 5% and 4.7%, or 0.3%.

So, "credit enhancement" isn't just some slick Wall Street terminology. Rather, it is a term that covers methods and mechanisms to lower interest rates (and lengthen term) by improving the credit rating on your project.

When financing projects, the goal is to drive down cost. As such you should consider any of these credit enhancement strategies that will help.

First and foremost, as has been expressed several times in this book, avoid using equity if at all possible because it is so expensive. Second, use lock boxes and liens. Third, divide your financing into tranches. Fourth, look for external guaranty or debt insurance funds. Fifth, look for a creditworthy government willing to guaranty the financing. Sixth, check out whether financial guaranty insurance is available and whether it is cost effective to buy it.

Always remember that the overarching goal is to provide the greatest environmental benefit to the largest number of people at the lowest possible cost. Credit enhancement is a means of achieving that goal.

Chapter 8—Old Water/ New Water

Early on in this book, we discussed the fact that in the middle of the 20th century, the country and the world were just beginning to wake up to the problem of pollution in general, and water pollution, in particular. At that time, urban sewage was the #1 cause of water pollution.

The United States finally got its act together in 1972 when the CWA was passed over the veto of President Nixon. The CWA contained a funding provision called the construction grant program. It was to be administered by EPA that had—oddly enough—been created by President Nixon in December 1970 by executive order. Over the next 15 years, EPA handed out over $70 billion of funds appropriated by Congress. These grants were made to local governments or authorities for sewer projects. They required a local match. So between the federal grants and the local matching funds, the United States spent well over $100 billion controlling urban water pollution between 1972 and 1987. And, as is often said, back in the 1970s and 1980s, $100 billion was real money.

By 1987, EPA had noticed that the grants, or "free money," had begotten some unfortunate side effects. These were overbuilding, "gilding" (using unnecessarily expensive fixtures), and dependency. Everyone wanted more. Everyone wanted their Uncle Sam to take care of them. No more. And so, in 1987, Congress made a wholesale amendment to the CWA and replaced the construction grant program with a loan program called the CWSRF. This program involved EPA's awarding of grants to the states, but the states could not pass on the grants to the local governments and authorities. They could only lend them the money. No grants; only loans. There are other financial powers that the CWSRFs have, like guarantees, purchase of local obligations, and investments; but loans are the most popular.

In addition, in 1996, Congress enacted the Safe Drinking Water Act (SDWA), which created the Drinking Water State Revolving Fund (DWSRF). In the 50 states plus Puerto Rico, the DWSRF and the CWSRF are managed by the same agencies. (Henceforth in this book, the CWSRF and the DWSRF in the states will be collectively referred to as the SRFs.)

The CWA Amendments did not specify a minimum interest rate at which the states could lend the money. So, to soften the blow of no more "free money," at the beginning of the program many of the 51 SRFs made their loans at a 0% interest rate. If you can't get the money for free, a loan at a 0% interest rate is the next best thing.

In the 30-years since the CWA Amendments passed, the 51 CWSRFs have provided over $125 billion of federal assistance for local water pollution control projects. In addition to financing projects for urban sewer agencies and authorities, the CWA Amendments also specified that SRF loans could be made for nonpoint source pollution control projects. Notwithstanding the new language about nonpoint source projects, the 51 SRFs have sunk 96% of their $125+ billion of funds into traditional urban sewage treatment projects. So, the SRFs became the bankers for the wastewater industry.

In addition, since 1996, the DWSRFs have received over an additional $20 billion for safe drinking water systems.

This strategy was wildly successful! On the DWSRF side, communities were able to provide their ratepayers with high quality drinking water at reasonable prices. And on the CWSRF side, urban sewage was the #1 source of water pollution. So, the country put its money right where the problem was. The 15 years of the construction grant program and the 30 years of the CWSRF focusing 96% of their efforts on urban sewage really worked. Today, almost 50 years later, urban sewage is no longer the #1 cause of water pollution.

Today, the #1 cause of water pollution is agricultural runoff, followed closely by stormwater. Both of these are nonpoint sources. Stormwater is regulated by the CWA, but most agricultural runoff is not. There is a type of NPDES permit for stormwater called a municipal separate storm sewer system (MS4) permit. MS4 permits, however, are issued to municipal governments not individual sources of stormwater pollution. Most states issue MS4 permits to local jurisdictions, which must implement stormwater flow reductions as the permit requires.

As you might guess, the CWSRFs are ill prepared to switch their efforts from point sources like urban sewage to problems on farms in the country and on churches, shopping malls and other sources of stormwater in the cities. The SRFs are accustomed to writing $3 million checks to wastewater agencies for new sewer mains. They have little experience lending $15,000 to farmers to plant locust trees on the banks of a stream that runs through their farm fields. That is one of the major reasons why "paying for tomorrow" will be substantially different than paying for the last 50 years. Not only will "paying for tomorrow" be very, very different, it will also be considerably more expensive.

Many communities have faced their MS4 problems by imposing some sort of fees on properties that contribute to stormwater flows. The press calls these fees "rain taxes." Stormwater fees are a good idea if they are broad based or statewide. Local stormwater fees have two issues. First, stormwater problems and money are not coincident. In Maryland there is the city of Baltimore with massive stormwater problems, but no money. A few miles to the northwest is the fifth richest county in the United States, which has only modest stormwater problems by comparison. The second issue is that many jurisdictions have based their rain tax on the square footage of impermeable surface on a given property. Furthermore, if you remediate the problem on your property, you can get a reduction in the rain tax you have to pay. The issue here is that the punishment doesn't fit the crime. Let's say that you are paying a $500 per year rain tax on your property. But if you tear up your driveway and replace it with permeable pavement you can get a $250 reduction in your rain tax, which is a savings to you. The only problem is that the new driveway might cost $15,000. So you spend $15,000 to save $250—not a recipe for success.

Although urban sewage is no longer our #1 water pollution problem, it is still a major problem. All of those facilities that we bought with the construction grant program's $100 billion and the CWSRFs $125 billion are now somewhere between 1 and 45 years old. Sewage treatment facilities and equipment have long service lives; but they are not infinite. They eventually wear out and have to be replaced. Many of the facilities and much of the equipment that was bought 30-40 years ago now needs replacing. Some urban water mains are over 100 years old. Plus, the population will not be static. People aren't going to stop having babies. And the babies will grow up and people will build new homes for them to live in. These new houses will need drinking water and sewer services.

So, we are not finished with "gray" infrastructure projects for urban sewer authorities. We will have to replace what is there now and we will have to build more for a growing population.

So, we will have all of these traditional projects to pay for in the coming tomorrows. They won't be cheap. Everything costs more today than it did 50 years ago. In 2015, EPA released a report that estimated $655 billion of traditional drinking water and wastewater projects would be needed in the next decade, just for replacements and to meet the needs of a growing population. Mind you, EPA's report only covered the next decade!

In 2016, the AWWA issued a report entitled, "Buried No Longer: Confronting America's Water Infrastructure." This report says that over $1 trillion is needed for just drinking water infrastructure in the next 25 years. The American Society of Civil Engineers (ASCE) agreed, giving the U.S. government a "D+" grade on its "Infrastructure Report Card."

These infrastructure "needs" numbers, however, should be put into perspective.

The annual trading volume of municipal bonds in the United States is some $3.7 trillion. That's trillion, not billion. This market supplies about 90% of the funds needed for water and wastewater infrastructure. Even with the recession of 2008, there are between $300 and $400 billion dollars of new municipal bonds each year. Water and wastewater infrastructure comprise about 10% of this number, so between $30 and $40 billion each year. According to Thompson Reuters Data, over $36 billion of tax exempt bonds were issued for water and wastewater projects in 2012. In addition, the CWSRF contributes another $7 billion and the DWSRF another $2.5 billion annually. So, overall there are existing sources of funding that provide $40-$50 billion *a year*. This means that between the municipal bond market and the two SRFs, the AWWA's numbers are relatively doable over the next 25-30 years. That's the good news. The bad news is that those numbers relate to the urban sewage problem only. And, of course, urban sewage is no longer the nation's #1 water pollution problem. Today, our #1 problem is a combination of agricultural runoff and stormwater. The above numbers barely scratch the surface of these two problems. So, "paying for tomorrow" in the water/wastewater sector will involve funding our current $40-$50 billion per year of traditional urban sewage problems, *but it will also mean that we have to start paying to clean up agricultural runoff and stormwater!* "Paying for tomorrow" will involve funding for far more than just urban infrastructure projects. We will also have to find a way to pay farmers to reduce agricultural runoff. And we will also have to pay many private-property owners in cities to install green infrastructure projects to mitigate the effects of stormwater.

Before we completely leave the subject of "urban sewage," we need to discuss yet another problem that will complicate "paying for tomorrow." We can illustrate this problem with a small story.

A gentleman who runs the SRF in a major southern state was asked if he would work on a couple of new finance concepts. He uncharacteristically declined. He said he didn't have the time. He said that there were several hundred small water systems in his state most of which needed major projects to maintain acceptable water quality. None of these systems had any money.

All of them were losing population. That's how the gentleman spent his time—working with these small poor systems with declining populations.

This is an issue we will have to deal with when "paying for tomorrow." Are we really going to ask these poor towns that are losing population to pay for rebuilding their half-century-old water works? If they don't pay for it, who will? Whom will we ask to pay for water projects for people who no longer live there or use the water system? Not a happy question. Spend money on people leaving town, or leave the people who hang around with bad water? Ouch!

One of the strategies for dealing with water/wastewater systems that are very small or have declining populations is consolidation.

When the country was being settled, every town had to have their own water system. It was a matter of pride. Taking people off drinking water wells and septic tanks and putting them on piped-in water/wastewater services meant that the town government worked. These services were provided by a local water and sewer authority. Each authority had a board of directors and a general manager. These officials were appointed either by the mayor, the town council, or both. It was a great honor to serve on the authority's board. This was a much sought after position, and so was the general manager position.

So the board members are distinguished local citizens. And the general manager is a well-respected man about town. In addition to being the general manager of the authority, he might also be the town postmaster. He might even tend bar in the evenings, just to make ends meet. So this is the organization that now is delivering inferior or contaminated water to its customers. It needs to upgrade its treatment plant. But it has no money. There are no jobs; so it can't raise rates. And because so many people have just left town, it's not even taking in enough revenue to pay all its bills.

To say that there are hundreds of small water systems in a state is a policymaker's nightmare. How totally inefficient! But there they are. Why not consolidate them? Give away the town water system? No mayor or town council wants to give away one of the town jewels. So, the "Podunk Water Authority" is here to stay.

Consolidation is a delicate word in the water industry. The National Rural Water Association (NRWA) deals with small water systems, ones that serve fewer than 10,000 people. The NRWA boasts a membership of some 31,000 rural water systems. Although you might think that the NRWA does not want to see its membership numbers shrink by consolidation, in fact it has assisted many small systems to consolidate where there is economy of scale and where the local utility fully supports it.

The National Association of Water Companies (NAWC) thinks consolidation is a holy word. This organization calls itself "the voice of private water" and, indeed, it is. NAWC's members include water companies that are so big that their shares are traded on the New York Stock Exchange. Like most private enterprises, "expansion" is part of these private water companies' vocabularies. So, how does a private water system "expand" in a given state? They expand by "taking over" other water systems. Their most likely candidates are the small systems without a lot of financial or technical expertise. NAWC members acquire other systems by purchasing them, by leasing them, or by contracting to operate them. When they do so, it's called by the politically correct term: "partnering." That's why the NAWC members think "consolidation" is a holy word.

Private water systems are not the only ones to take over other systems. Public systems and cooperative systems can do the same—although this is a rare phenomenon. Sometimes neighboring public systems will consolidate. But this doesn't happen very often either.

So, in cases where the authority itself and its distinguished board of directors are here to say, the solution is not abolishing the system or giving away the management, rather the solution lies with contracting another water institution to provide the services they need. They can hire outside operators, especially private ones like NAWC members. This can work. The town isn't going to give away its water authority. Instead, they can just consolidate operations by contract. Operational consolidation may well be the way of the future for rural American water systems.

Consolidation with a private company is a real option. Consolidating, however, with another public system is not so real. But there is an alternative.

Maryland has made two very gracious gifts to maintain the quality of life for the American people. First and foremost is the Bay Restoration Fund, or "flush tax," which you've already read about earlier in the book and will again later in this chapter. The second great gift is the Maryland Environmental Service (MES). Although you could easily be fooled into thinking that the MES was a private business, if you looked closely at their operations, the MES is a state agency. It looks like a business, but it is not. It was created in 1970 to provide environmental services for local governments that didn't provide their own. Today, among other chores, the MES manages/operates some 138 private, municipal, and county water and wastewater treatment plants and 90 more small systems in state-owned facilities like hospitals and prisons. The truly amazing thing about the MES is that it does not receive one penny from the Maryland state budget! The MES is paid for by its services. So if the MES is running your water system, every time you pay your monthly fee, you are paying it to the MES. The MES is entirely self-supporting! How good is the MES? Well, if it didn't do a good job, its 138 customers would certainly go elsewhere for expertise to run their utility plants.

Is the MES model a viable alternative in other states? Well, if you contract with a private company and you get into a dispute, you have to hire an expensive lawyer. If you have a problem with the MES, you call your state legislators. Since 1970, this system has worked very well. To date there is nothing like the MES in any other state. But as we start "paying for tomorrow," there may well be.

Now, on to the new #1 water pollution problem: agricultural runoff and stormwater.

In March 2015, the Des Moines Water Works filed a lawsuit against the drainage districts in three upstream counties. The problem was the high nitrate levels in the Raccoon River from which the city got its water. Des Moines sought damages and penalties. The suit contended that it cost the Des Moines Water Works some $1.2 million per year to remove the nitrates from the river, which is the source of drinking water for over 500,000 central Iowa residents. Des Moines said that an agricultural practice of using drainage tiles was the culprit. Tiles accelerate runoff of water from farm fields. Without tiles the water migrates more slowly and more of the nitrates are absorbed in the soil. So, tiles help farmers dry their fields out faster so they can get better crop yields, but the tiles empty the water, loaded with nitrates, into the nearest receiving water body, which, in this case, is the Raccoon River.

Less well known, but a far more important provision of the complaint was a request to have farms declared to be "point sources" of water pollution. This is an extremely radical position. Point sources of water pollution are strictly regulated by the CWA. Nonpoint sources are not regulated at all. Each point source must operate under an NPDES permit that specifies how much of each pollutant/nutrient it can emit. This means that if Des Moines had prevailed in their lawsuit that, theoretically, every farm in Iowa would become a point source of water pollution. Every farm would, therefore, have to be issued an NPDES permit! Permits for farmers? This is blasphemy! This is heresy! Regulate farms? Not in this country! Not in this century!

Although it was not their stated objective to do so, in 2015, EPA sought to regulate farms through the back door. The CWA says that EPA has jurisdiction over "the waters of the United States"; but it doesn't define this term. So, EPA and the U.S. Army Corps of Engineers (the Corps) promulgated a rule that said that "waters of the United States" included the tiny little streams, rivulets, and drainage ditches on farms. The agricultural community and the Farm Bureau went ballistic. They, of course, sued EPA. This story, however, has a happy ending. In November 2017, EPA and the Corps—under direct prodding from the Trump White House—have announced hearings on rescinding the rule.

The Des Moines lawsuit was dismissed in March 2017 on sovereign immunity grounds. So, the issues in the case were never decided. This means that the upstream farmers aren't going to pay for Des Moines water treatment and they aren't going to have to have NPDES permits for their farms. Des Moines Water Works has decided not to appeal the court's decision.

As we said, the huge infusion of money from the construction grant program and the SRF worked. Today urban sewage is no longer the #1 source of water pollution. Today agricultural runoff and stormwater are the #1 source of water pollution. This has caused two major problems.

First, the CWSRFs, having spent 96% of their $125 billion on POTWs, are used to making out $3+ million checks to wastewater agencies. They have little experience lending, say $50,000, to a farmer for a best management practice (BMP) that would reduce agricultural runoff.

The second problem is worse. When the CWSRFs loaned money to wastewater authorities, these agencies usually had tens of thousands—if not hundreds of thousands of ratepayers—over whom they could spread the cost. An upgrade to their treatment plant might cost $10 million. But they could borrow 100% of this money from their CWSRF at say, a 4% interest rate, for a term of 30 years. This would result in an annual payment of about $600,000. Now if the authority had 100,000 ratepayers (all paying equally), it would cost each one of them $6 per year or $0.50 per month.

Contrast this with a farmer who can build a constructed wetland on two acres of his land that he doesn't need for crops. This would certainly make a major reduction in the runoff from his farm. The wetland might cost $100,000. The farmer could also borrow from the CWSRF under the same terms and conditions as the POTW. His annual payment would be about $6,000, which is $500 a month. But, the only person he can spread this cost over with is himself. How many farmers are going to pay $6,000 per year to reduce water pollution out of the goodness of their hearts?

There is no legal authority in the CWA to require the farmer to do anything. He can simply go on polluting. This sounds like an ugly choice: keep polluting or pay $6,000 a year for the next 30 years. But in fact that is the way things are. And that is why "paying for tomorrow's clean water" has to be different.

The same situation is true with stormwater. Many wastewater utilities are saddled with the responsibility for reducing stormwater. The less precipitation a parcel of property absorbs, the more it exacerbates the urban stormwater problem. If the stormwater has no place to go, it heads for the nearest sewer or conduit where it joins countless more gallons of stormwater—usually in a sanitary sewer—all of which carry all of the pollutants from lawn fertilizer to animal waste to roadside garbage into the river or lake that receives the community's excess rain.

Properties that are impermeable create the worst stormwater problems. There are, however, new ways of dealing with impermeable land, called "green infrastructure." They basically replace concrete and cement with vegetation that absorbs rain as it falls. There are several popular types of green infrastructure.

Rainwater harvesting is one. This means catching rain in barrels. Instead of a downspout on the side of a house that just flushes rainwater onto some pavement, homeowners can either collect the rainwater and use it, e.g., for gardening, or they can simply empty it into the sewer after the storm passes and the stormwater flows have subsided.

Green roofs are another. In this case, the owner of a building replaces the tile on the flat roof of his building with a few inches of soil and some simple plants. These will absorb rainwater and keep it out of the sewer system.

Bioswales and retention ponds are another. Retention ponds hold stormwater during rain events, facilitate absorption by vegetation, and release it gradually into the sewer system. Bioswales have similar functions but are linear and convey stormwater while absorbing it. But the emphasis here is that bioswales and retention ponds are built on grass or other vegetation, instead of concrete. Both are commonly found adjacent to large parking lots or near shopping malls. Sometimes they are required as part of a building permit.

Rain gardens are another. A rain garden is basically a patch of vegetation. Often, concrete near a sidewalk or on a patio is simply torn up and replaced with grass and other vegetation. Again, the vegetation absorbs much of the rain.

Finally, there is another strategy that can be used for parking lots: permeable pavement. This is pavement that allows rain to percolate underground to the earth below. Again, it slows the flow of rainwater into the sewer system.

All of this said, when it comes to paying for green infrastructure in cities, we have the same problem that we have on the farm: much of it needs to be on private land. There are finance programs—the same ones available to farmers—but they are loan programs. And the loans must be paid back. And so, the same question arises: who is going to pay for the green infrastructure on private property? The owner?

In some cities, there may well be landowners that are forced to build green infrastructure on their property. Think of a large industrial facility with a huge parking lot. Or think of a shopping mall with tens of thousands of feet of concrete. These enterprises arguably have the funds to pay for green infrastructure on their properties.

All well and good, but, putting it a different way, what governor or mayor is going to tell the pastor of a large urban church that he must tear up his concrete parking lot and replace it with, say, $50,000 of permeable pavement? And that he must take the money to pay for the permeable pavement out of the Sunday collection plate? No mayor I know!

The point here is that "paying for tomorrow's" clean water is going to be different than "paying for today," or at least, "paying for the past." In addition to paying for the modernization and expansion of urban water and wastewater facilities, we will also be paying for agricultural runoff reduction projects on farmland and we will be paying for green infrastructure project in cities on private land as well.

In Chapter 2, we discussed five strategies for devising new payment systems for agricultural runoff and green infrastructure.

Again, they are:

1. "Adoption." where downstream customers and ratepayers of an urban sewer authority pay for upstream farmers to install runoff reduction projects. The ratepayers of the downstream sewer authority "adopt" the farmer's upstream project.

2. "Sponsorship." This is where a state's CWSRF absorbs the cost of the upstream project that is "sponsored" by a downstream authority or other institution. As you might imagine, the CWSRF cannot do this indefinitely or at a large scale.

3. "Nutrient credit trading" where agencies or institutions that have NPDES permit problems and need nutrient credits to satisfy the requirements of those permits. In this case, they would pay the farmer to undertake a runoff project in return for the credits he would earn for doing so.

4. Regional or watershed fees or charges.

Chapter 8: Old Water/New Water

5. Statewide fees or charges.

Suffice it to say that the use of none of these strategies is commonplace. They are all in their relative infancy for the simple reason that people have been worrying about urban sewage for the last half century.

"Adoption" requires the goodwill and cooperation of the state's environmental regulatory agency. Even though it saves them money, "sponsorship" projects require the goodwill and cooperation of a major sewer authority as well as the CWSRF, which winds up paying for the "sponsored" project.

"Nutrient credit trading" is even more problematic. No two parcels of farmland are identical. Different crops, different topography, different soil, different uses of fertilizers, different farming practices, etc. For this reason, flat out statements such as "the runoff from 100 acres of corn contains 3,000 pounds of nitrogen" don't exist. No scientist or soil engineer would make such a definitive statement. Serious amounts of time and energy on the part of farmers are required before anyone has any idea how many nutrient credits any particular project might generate. Why should a farmer spend this time and energy without knowing, at the end of the game, that he would have a meaningful amount of credits to sell at an attractive price? That's why, at this stage in its evolution, nutrient trading is too idiosyncratic to be a common practice. As noted in Chapter 2, the GAO found that only one state, Pennsylvania, has a trading system involving the private sector, and even that program is far from robust.

"Regional or watershed fees" are also a relatively new phenomenon. Here we are referring to funds that in no way are connected to sewer authorities. They are independent funds.

Watershed protection is becoming a major issue in the water industry (again because urban sewage is taking a back seat). So, there are some water agencies that have instituted fees or charges to their customers, the proceeds from which are used for watershed protection projects. These charges are simply tacked onto the bill. For example, the Beaver Water District is a major utility in northwest Arkansas. The district owns Beaver Lake and sells the lake water wholesale to nearby water districts that resell the water at retail to homes and businesses. The district has taken several steps to protect the quality of the lake water. Principally, they have bought up adjacent land to prevent it from being developed. So, the eventual ratepayers pay for these projects, but they do so very indirectly.

Strategies like this are all well and good, but the type of regional or watershed fees or charges we are referring to here are those that are managed independently of any water of sewer agency. These independent funds are created by one or another unit of government. The money in these funds comes from fees, charges, or taxes that are imposed by the government or agency. They are like the two watershed funds in North Carolina that are described in Chapter 2. These funds should be available for any type of project that improves or protects the water in the watershed area. They should be available for agricultural runoff projects and for green infrastructure. They should also be available for traditional watershed protection projects, like land acquisition, as well.

"Statewide fees" are the big brothers or sisters of regional/watershed funds. As the name plainly says, the fees or charges involved with these funds are charges as broadly as is politically possible on a statewide basis. The word "political" is a key word with these statewide funds. Statewide funds will require state legislation. And state legislation will require political goodwill from all sectors of society in order to be passed.

As noted in Chapter 2, these funds should have several very important characteristics.

First, they should plainly say what the money is going to be used for. Maryland's "Bay Restoration Fund" is a great example. When a Maryland residents open their tax bills or sewer bills and see the fund listed, they know exactly what they are paying for—their beloved Chesapeake Bay. Another excellent attribute of this fund is that it is very broad based. It was originally based on the number of toilets in a building. Because of this, the local news media refer to the Bay Restoration Fee as the "flush tax." Now, that's what everyone in Maryland calls it, except the politicians! And that is also good because when people pay their "flush tax" they know exactly what they are paying for. Both the Bay Restoration Fee and the flush tax are great names.

The second important characteristic is that the fee is as broad based as possible. Everyone pollutes. Everyone enjoys the benefits of clean water. So, everyone should pay.

The third important characteristic is that the fee should be reasonable. It should not be painful for the public to pay.

The flush tax, for example, is very reasonable. In 2004, when it was created, it was $2.50 per month per household. In 2012, the flush tax was doubled to $5 per month with barely a whimper from the public.

The flush tax is used to pay debt service on bonds issued to pay for POTW projects that needed doing immediately. But the state is slowly expanding the purposes for which the flush tax can be used.

Unfortunately, as of this writing, Maryland's "Bay Restoration Fee" is the only statewide fund in the country.

So, the Maryland flush tax is truly ingenious and truly deserves emulation by other states.

Adoption and sponsorship are essentially temporary fixes on the payment problem. Nutrient trading may eventually work and be important. But in terms of "paying for tomorrow," fees and charges, whether regional or statewide are the real way to pay for clean water.

The fourth and final important characteristic of environmental fees is to make the uses or purposes of these funds as broad as possible. They should be used to reduce any kind of pollution. Not just agricultural runoff. Not effluent from POTWs. Not just stormwater. Any form of water pollution!

So, "paying for tomorrow" in the water world will involve our continuing to pay for the "gray infrastructure" to replace or update the urban sewage treatment facilities that we built many years ago. It will also involve our paying for the new "green infrastructure" that we need to reduce the polluting effects of stormwater. Finally, it will involve our biting the bullet and approving new fees or charges—at least regional, if not statewide—to raise the funds to pay for agricultural runoff.

So, we know what we need to do to have clean water for tomorrow. And we will surely be "paying for that tomorrow."

Chapter 9—Old Air/New Air

As you have read several times already in this book, when the United States got serious about water pollution, we passed the CWA, a major part of which was the "construction grant program." Over the next 15 years, this program pumped over $70 billion into sewage treatment plants POTWs as they are called. With the state match, there was over $100 billion spent, and that was followed by the CWSRF with another $125+ billion for water pollution.

No such thing happened in the air sector. Congress did not appropriate a penny of financial assistance to reduce air pollution.

Fortunately, the United States never suffered a "Great Smog" event like London did back in 1952. But we had our own problems. Our major cities like Chicago, Los Angeles, and New York were choked by emissions from coal-burning furnaces and vehicles. In those days, many private homes were heated by coal-burning furnaces. Smog from cars and trucks was the constant subject of television news stories that featured the drastic reductions in visibility that smog was causing on freeways and other major arteries.

In addition to domestic coal furnaces and vehicle emissions, there were industrial furnaces too. These are the sources of pollution that the CAA addressed.

Whereas the CWA attacked water pollution with money and grants, the CAA attacked air pollution with regulations. The reason for these two disparate strategies stems from the respective sources of pollution. People—men, women, and children—are the sources of the human waste that made up the urban sewage polluting the nation's waterways. On the other hand, organizations—both public and private—were the sources of air emissions. You can't regulate human waste; but the government can certainly regulate organizations. They can regulate businesses and they can regulate entities like schools, hospitals, and other public institutions including their own government offices.

These laws were very successful. The nation's major water bodies are much cleaner. The $225 billion we spent produced excellent results. Our air is cleaner too. Vehicular emissions have ceased to be a major air pollution problem except on the West Coast where the effect of vehicular emissions is exacerbated by natural climatic conditions. As of today, the six most heavily polluted cities in the United States are in California. Vehicular emissions can be dealt with easily by regulation. But the government didn't need to regulate drivers. They could regulate vehicles at their source—automobile manufacturers. The cost of vehicle emission controls are buried in the overall price of a car. It was almost as painless as paying a sewer bill.

If these statutes were so successful at dealing with our pollution issues, what is the problem now?

If a factory or industrial facility emits smoke, it has to have a permit. Permits are very specific. They detail how much of each type of pollutant a business or institution can emit into the air. Permits almost always required a reduction in emissions. This meant that the business had to buy and install new equipment to scrub the air before it was emitted. The equipment was expensive. Since it usually did not add one penny of productive capacity to the business, it was a pure financial burden on the owner who had to pay for the pollution abatement equipment himself. No grants. No loans. No financial assistance of any kind. So, whereas the CWA provided billions of dollars to clean up water pollution, there was no comparable provision in the CAA.

Those were the air pollution problems that we successfully addressed in the CAA.

The new air pollution issues we face *today* are far more subtle.

Our now-traditional regulatory approach to air pollution from private industry and businesses has taken a new and complicated turn. This situation is getting new scrutiny.

Fifty years ago, jobs and economic development were not a political issue. In those days, few, if any, state or local governments had offices or departments of economic development. When I was young, I worked for the New York State Department of Commerce. Note that it was not then called "the Department of Economic Development." The Department of Commerce was created in 1941. It was years later, in 1987—when jobs became a hot political issue—that the state legislature changed the name to the Department of Economic Development. Today, economic development, or "jobs," is a major political issue. Politicians have to talk about creating and maintaining jobs, and then they have to put in policies that are business– and industry–friendly. As a result, state and local governments have to be careful about imposing costly air pollution control requirements on industries. If the cost of compliance is too high, some of those industries might just pick up and head for a less zealous jurisdiction. If so, the community loses all of those valuable jobs. And the politician might lose his job as well.

Chapter 9: Old Air/New Air

As I said in the Introduction to this book, when I was a boy in Buffalo, New York, the poster child of air pollution was a steel mill in the adjacent city of Lackawanna to the South. Lackawanna was a dump. The Lackawanna Steel plant, later the Bethlehem Steel plant, was built on the shore of Lake Erie. The city of Lackawanna was built inland from the plant, which meant that it was downwind of the plant. This means that every day the city of Lackawanna was blanketed with stinking black smoke from the steel plant.

The ending to this Buffalo story is not happy. In 1983 the plant closed. I am certain that the financial burden of complying with air pollution regulations had something to do with the closing decision. But I think the dominant reason was wholesale changes in the economics of steel making in the United States. Since then the property has been rehabilitated into a pleasant lakeshore area. No more black smoke.

The unhappy aspect of the plant closing was the economic development impact. It was the jobs, the people, the workers. In its heyday the plant employed some 25,000 souls. They are now gone. So, in terms of jobs and economic development, the Bethlehem Steel story is a disaster.

So, what is the poor politician supposed to do? Adopt lax industrial pollution standards, keep the jobs, but face the wrath of an electorate choking on bad air; or vigorously enforce stringent air pollution regulations and suffer the wrath of an electorate hungry for jobs?

Industrial air pollution is an old problem that now has a new face. It may well be time that the government introduces a little money into the air pollution game as it has done for water pollution.

Think of a business facing an air pollution regulation requiring installation of new equipment costing about $1 million. Let's say that the equipment has a service life of 30 years. The business owner can go out and write a check for $1 million (if he has that much) and be done with it. Or, maybe he can go to his bank and get a five-year loan at 8%. The annual payment on that loan would be $250,456. So his choices are to pay $1 million today, or $250,456 for the next five years, or move 50 miles to a different state where he wouldn't have to buy the equipment or pay anything. Who knows what the owner would really do? But moving out of state is clearly an attractive option.

Let's say 1,000 jobs are at stake, but the governor and state legislature are strongly "pro job." What could they do?

Well, the state could set up a financial assistance program along the lines of the CWSRF. If they did that the state would be able to offer the business owner a $1 million loan for 30 years at a 4% interest rate. The annual payment on this loan would be $57,830. Much better than paying $1 million today. Much better than making the bank loan payment of $250,456. Would the owner keep his business in the state, or move out of state. Well with a payment of only $57,830 instead of $250,456, he is that much more likely to stay. So, mission accomplished: the jobs remain in state and the air regulation is enforced!

How much would this $1 million cost the state? The answer is: nothing. Not a penny. The state would issue $1 million of 30-year, tax-exempt bonds at an interest rate of 4%. They would simply pass the money through to the business owner. The state could assure itself of repayment by placing a tax lien on the owner's premises.

So, in terms of "paying for tomorrow," as the states become more involved in the jobs issue, and as air controls get more stringent, we may very well see states setting up financial assistance programs for air pollution control equipment for privately owned firms.

So, that is how the old game will change. Financial assistance will be added to enforcement as a compliance tool.

In addition to changes in the old game, there is a new game in the air business that has to do with climate change, global warming, and GHGs. This all has to do with the earth getting hotter—global warming. Paying for global warming will also be part of "paying for tomorrow."

Most people know that there have been several ice ages. These are periods when the earth cools off and snow and ice cover large areas. Between the ice ages, the earth warms up. That is what is happening now. The earth is naturally warming.

To this, however, are added anthropogenic GHGs. These are chemicals that are produced by human beings that trap the sun's heat in the atmosphere. CO_2, methane, nitrous oxide, ozone, chloroflurocarbons, and hydrofluorocarbons are the principal anthropogenic greenhouse gases. They accelerate the warming of the planet. Since the beginning of the Industrial Revolution in the mid-18th century, humans have caused a 40% increase in CO_2 in the atmosphere. Humans contribute about 30 billion tons a year of CO_2. These gases remain in the atmosphere, so that their effect is cumulative.

Most of the CO_2 that we contribute comes from the burning of fossil fuels at electric power-generating stations. GHGs emitted by power plants are regulated by the states. The impact of these regulations—like the installation of air scrubbers—is reflected in our utility bills.

So, what are we to do? We've got to have electricity.

In the Introduction to this book I recounted an event that happened with one of my students from Copenhagen. Denmark gets the majority of its

Chapter 9: Old Air/New Air

power from wind. He and I compared the cost of home energy between his parents' apartment in Copenhagen and mine in Maryland. We were both paying about the same amount of money. But in Maryland, I was paying $0.09 per kwh. In Copenhagen, his parents were paying $0.37 per kwh. The cost of power in Denmark was four times higher than in Maryland! Or to put it in a much more telling light, I was using over four times the power that my student's parents were using!

There are two lessons here. The first is to replace fossil fuel-generated electricity with energy from renewable sources, like wind. The second point is even more important: conservation! The student's parents were using much less power that I was. This is the way of the future. In the air business we have to incentivize the conservation of energy and the use of renewables. We Americans tend to be profligate in our use of electricity. It's not expensive, so we use vast quantities of it—far more than we should.

There is another lesson tucked into the above example, but it's not evident to the naked eye. The price of many types of renewable energy is coming down, the more we use it. The price of solar panels has dropped 60% in the last five years. Solar is so popular that it is definitely seeing economies of scale.

So, there is definitely some good news about "paying for tomorrow" in the energy sector. Renewable energy is environmentally safe. Its price is coming down. The price of electricity from fossil fuels is going up. This is largely so because some states are putting taxes or fees onto our electric bills to partially compensate for the pollution caused by burning fossil fuels.

Carbon taxes, per se, have not been adopted in the United States. They have in several countries like the Australia, Ireland, Sweden, and the United Kingdom. It is unlikely that they will be adopted in the United States, at least at the national level, during the Trump Administration.

There is, however, an ingenious fundraising mechanism that has been adopted by nine states in the Northeast. This mechanism is called the Regional Greenhouse Gas Initiative (RGGI). The nine states involved are: Connecticut, Delaware, Maine, Maryland, Massachusetts, New Hampshire, New York, Rhode Island, and Vermont. It is not a carbon tax in the strict sense, but it functions like one. Here's how it works.

The RGGI states have inventoried the electric power-generating stations above 25 megawatts in size in their region that burn fossil fuel. They then set a regional limit for carbon emissions from these plants. These power plants must buy carbon credits from RGGI. So, RGGI auctions off the credits and the electric power companies buy them.

Now, the shareholders of these power companies do not eat the cost of the credits. On the contrary, the power companies pass along the cost of the credits to their customers. Now, doesn't this look like a carbon tax? The customers are paying so that their electricity provider can continue to burn fossil fuels and emit carbon.

The nine states share the money that the auction produces. The good thing is that the states use these funds to promote energy efficiency and renewable energy projects.

So, when it comes to air pollution, what will we be "paying for tomorrow"? One of the answers is that as politicians try to reconcile jobs with environmental air controls, there are likely to be new programs. The good aspect of such policies is the cost: nothing! As noted above, states can borrow the money in the municipal bond market and then re-lend it at the same rate to companies purchasing air pollution control equipment. No private businesses can borrow for, say, 20 years at a 4% interest rate. So the states could even add on a small administrative fee for themselves.

On the climate change issue, we will continue to pay more for power generated from fossil fuels. But, we can at least partially offset these increases with conservation. We must learn to use less electricity.

The final piece of good news is that the more we replace energy from fossil fuels with renewable energy, the less that renewable energy will cost.

Chapter 10—Resilience and Cybersecurity

This chapter deals with two issues. The first is "resilience," which deals with paying for some of the consequences of climate change or global warming.

The second issue is "cybersecurity," which involves protecting the power grid that supplies the country with electricity. Our power system in this country is vulnerable, very vulnerable. But, what does cybersecurity have to do with our quality of life? The consequences of major destruction of the country's electric power grid would have catastrophic consequences on the lives of all Americans.

Resilience is the stepchild of global warming. It is essentially how to survive global warming. New words—like mitigation and adaptation, and resilience itself—have come to be used to describe strategies for avoiding consequences of global warming. These strategies cost money to implement. They need new financial mechanisms to be cost effective. They could also benefit from a new legal regime that could marshal the resources necessary to deal with global warming.

Global warming will have different impacts depending on location. Some areas of the planet will become uninhabitable because they will be too hot to grow crops for food. Other areas will become habitable for the first time. You will be able to buy beachfront property on the Arctic Ocean and open a surfing school.

The first part of this chapter discusses how coastal resiliency projects, in specific, can be financed by states. Coastal resilience addresses rising sea levels, as well as severe waves generated by extreme weather events. The second part of the chapter deals with the concept of an "interstate compact" as a legal mechanism to help the states both "to adapt to" and "to mitigate" some of the effects of global warming.

To deal with the finance issue, coastal resiliency projects need to be divided into their logical categories so that the various financing options for each type of project can be examined.

Coastal resiliency projects can be divided into two groups. The first group involves beach replenishment, dune building, and also back-bay and small inlet dredging. These projects protect coastal communities from serious storm damage. We can call this group "disaster mitigation" projects.

"Post-disaster resiliency" projects are a second and very specific category. This category involves the reconstruction of ONLY the core economic drivers (CEDs) of a community. For example, many coastal communities rely on tourism for their economic existence. Therefore, the CEDs in that community are those specific amenities that attract tourists. Beaches are CEDs. So are boardwalks. So are the "beachy" shops on the boardwalks. So are amusement parks and other entertainment facilities.

Providing for the rebuilding of CEDs is not a general replacement for flood insurance. Rather it is a replacement program for only the CEDs in coastal communities that are destroyed by hurricanes or other extreme weather events. Using Ocean City, Maryland, as an example, post-disaster resiliency projects would include: reconstruction of the beach, reconstruction of the boardwalk, reconstruction of the stores on the boardwalk, and reconstruction of recreational facilities such as the amusement parks. In short, the CEDs are the facilities that lure visitors to the coastal community. They are the facilities that need to be rebuilt immediately after a storm—with no delays and no hassles—in order to get the community's economy going again.

Among the financial issues discussed will be a system benefit charge model, special districts, seasonal charges, and geographically targeted charges. The concept involved in both the seasonal charges and the geographically targeted charges is to draw revenues for coastal resiliency from those who use and enjoy the coasts and who, otherwise, don't contribute to their well-being. Public-private partnerships (P3s) can also play a role in financing resiliency projects. P3s, however, have a much larger role in financing. They will be discussed in Chapter 11.

Below are some alternative means of financing these projects.

The System Benefit Charge Model

This model addresses three essential strategies for protecting oceanside communities: beach replenishment, dune rebuilding, and channel dredging. Strong beach structures protect communities from storm surges and high waves. The same is true of dunes, which protect inland property. Dredging has a critical role in flood mitigation.

This model presents one possible mechanism for financing pre-hurricane fortification programs to replenish beaches, rebuild dunes, and dredge criti-

Chapter 10: Resilience and Cybersecurity

cal channels. The assumption underlying these concepts is that these programs must be carried out every four years. This means that 25% of the money necessary should be raised each year. It also means that the use of long-term municipal bonds is not feasible.

The central concept behind this finance mechanism is that the fortification programs protect the economies of beachfront communities. What good is it to harden water, sewer, cables, gas, and electric utilities if the businesses that use these services are destroyed? No businesses, no jobs, no communities.

Gas and electric utilities, together with state public utility commissions, have taken the lead in making their facilities resilient. Many states have added system benefit charges (SBCs) to the electricity bills of consumers. These charges were originally designed to provide funds for utilities to assist their residential customers in installing energy efficiency measures such as home insulation, modern HVAC, modern electric appliances, etc. But lately, many electric utilities have applied to their respective state public utility boards for permission to use these funds for hardening, or resiliency, programs. In New York, ConEdison has mounted an over $1 billion hardening program in the five boroughs of New York City alone. This program is financed by SBCs.

This existing SBC/hardening concept can be expanded to pay for fortification strategies, especially beach replenishment and dune replacement that will protect entire communities from hurricanes. In a sense, it will be an extension of each utility's own hardening program.

In short, each utility will be asked to pay a share of the quadrennial cost of implementing these fortification programs, a charge that will be passed along to their individual users according to their individual use.

Here is how such a system might work:

(Wherever possible, data below has been taken from the state of Maryland, and/or Ocean City, Maryland, or Worcester County, where Ocean City is located.)

Water & Sewer—A 2010 survey by the AWWA done by Raftelis reported that the average combined water and sewer bill for households was 1.5% of MHI. In Maryland the MHI is $69,272. In Worcester County, it is $55,487. So, the combined water/sewer charges for homes in Worcester County are, putatively, around $830 per year.

Electricity—According to the Energy Information Administration (EIA) the average residential electricity bill in Maryland in 2012 was $129 per month, or $1,548 per year. The EIA has no breakdown by county.

Natural Gas—According to the American Gas Association, the average annual residential gas bill in Maryland in 2012 was $760.

Telephone—According to the Federal Communications Commission, the average charge for a basic landline is about $30 per month. With state and local taxes and charges, this comes to about $50 per month, or $600 per year.

Cable TV—According to Forbes, the national average cable bill in 2011 was $86 per month and is expected to rise to $123 by next year. So, let us use $115 per month, or $1,380 per year.

In summary, here's what these charges look like on an annual basis:

Water & Sewer	$830	16%
Electricity	$1,548	30%
Natural Gas	$760	15%
Telephone	$600	12%
Cable TV	$1,380	27%
Total	$5,118	100%

Now, let's say (again putting volumetric considerations aside) that the average household, as described above vis-à-vis its utility usage, needs to pay $400 for its share of the fortification programs. On an annual basis this would be $100.

So, in this case the $100 annual charge would be distributed across the five utility bills as follows:

Charges	%	Year	Month
Water & Sewer	16%	$16	$1.34
Electricity	30%	$30	$2.50
Natural Gas	15%	$15	$1.25
Telephone	12%	$12	$1
Cable TV	27%	$27	$2.25
Total	100%	$100	$8.33

As you can see, what might be called the "SBC approach" does have the benefit of spreading out these costs over several revenue sources, making paying for them less painful.

As it turns out, however, using Ocean City/Worcester County as an example raises some serious collateral problems. Worcester County is home to 100% of Maryland's Atlantic shoreline that runs 31 miles. It is also home to less than 1% of Maryland's population. So we have a large "per capita/beach" issue in Worcester County, Maryland. Presumably, there are other areas along the coast, like Atlantic City, New Jersey, where this ratio is more manageable.

Another problem with the SBC approach in Worcester County is that whereas Maryland is the richest state in the Union with a MHI of $69,272, Worcester County's MHI is only $55,487, which is 20% below the state average. So there is an equity issue here as well. But the SBC model serves very well as a funding mechanism for fortification programs based on utility use as a surrogate for economic importance. In other words, the more electricity a home or business uses, the higher would be its utility bill and the charge for the fortification programs that protect it.

Special Districts

One finance mechanism for rebuilding a community's CED would be a multi-state disaster insurance policy. The key concept here is that a Category 5 hurricane cannot make a direct hit everywhere in a multi-state area. This argues for a regional approach to spread the risk of loss over a wide geographic area. This regional approach to major disasters can be effectuated by the creation of an interstate compact. The more landmass there is in an insurance program, the greater the spread of risk, the lower the cost of the premiums. So, for the Mid-Atlantic, Virginia through Massachusetts might be considered.

So, the key idea here is to create an insurance fund—in the private sector—that will be used to rebuild a community's economic core if it is destroyed in a major hurricane.

Here is how such a private disaster insurance finance program might be organized in a time sequence.

First, each state would ask its "at risk" communities to determine which public and private facilities are critical to their local economy, i.e, which constitute their CED. Using Ocean City, Maryland, as an example, one would certainly think of the beach—above all—and then the boardwalk. Then the businesses on the boardwalk. Then the amusement park and other amusement facilities. Then any other enterprise that would prominently appear on an analysis of sales tax revenues for the area. The communities would be asked to estimate the cost of replacement for each, assuming they were completely destroyed by a hurricane.

Second, the individual states would review these reconstruction plans and their associated costs and, ultimately, approve them.

Third, the states would collectively do the same, i.e., approve each other's plans and associated costs. Once this is done, eligibility issues should be finished. The facilities to be rebuilt in each community will have been decided upon. What remains then is a map of the participating states with price tags representing the rebuilding costs on each participating community.

Hurricane Sandy was the second most expensive hurricane in history. The official price tag was $68 billion. So, let's say that an "average" hurricane would cost $40 billion. Le's also say that out of this total cost, rebuilding the key core businesses would comprise a 10%, or $4 billion. So, this would be the face amount of the insurance policy.

Fifth, once the face amount of the policy had been determined, the insurance companies would be asked to quote a premium for that (maximum) amount of coverage.

Sixth, once the bids are in, the participating states would select the insurer.

Seventh, now the piper must be paid. We now know how much premium needs to be paid; but we don't know who will pay and how much they each will pay.

"Who" and "how much" are policy questions that will ultimately be answered by the participating states. But here is one variation that might be considered.

The payment scheme that we will use here, as an example, will be based on the economics of hurricane destruction. It will also be based, to a degree, on the National Flood Insurance Program's policy of breaking up areas into zones of probable damage. It will involve the creation of Special Disaster Districts. Finally, it will also involve the imposition of annual *ad valorem* charges on real property to pay the premium.

It should be noted that there are other mechanisms that could be used to finance the premium, including value capture mechanisms such as Tax Increment Districts. But the most reliable of all of these is a Special Tax District (STD) where the income is constant and does not fluctuate from year to year.

Using the State of Maryland again as an example, we could break it down into 4 "Special Disaster Districts." The first would be the Maximum Impact Zone. In our example, this is Ocean City and other such highly vulnerable communities. Next would be High Impact Zone with coastal communities such as Cambridge and other vulnerable coastal areas. Next would be Low Impact Zones like Salisbury. Next would be the Economic Impact Zone,

Chapter 10: Resilience and Cybersecurity

which would be the remainder of the state and would be based on the theory that the loss of income from NOT rebuilding Ocean City would cause the rest of the state economic harm.

Now, Maryland's landmass is 10,455 square miles, which is 6,691,200 acres. Let's assume an average assessed value of $10,000 per acre on all acreage. That is $66,912,000,000 of value. Call it $67 billion.

Now let us assume that the participating states decide to purchase $4 billion of catastrophe insurance and that Maryland would use 10% of that coverage, or $400 million.

Now let's assume that the coverage to premium ratio is 20:1, which means that the annual premium is 1/20th of the $4 billion cover, or $200 million.

Maryland's share of this premium would be 10% of $200 million, or $20 million.

Let's say that Maryland draws a map showing the following acreage in each of its disaster zones:

Zone	% Acreage	Acres
Maximum Impact	3%	200,736
High Impact	7%	468,384
Low Impact	15%	1,003,680
Economic Impact	75%	5,018,400

Let's also say that Maryland determines the following distribution of premium costs by zone:

Zone	% of Premium	Premium
Maximum Impact	40%	$8 million
High Impact	30%	$6 million
Low Impact	20%	$4 million
Economic Impact	10%	$2 million

Under this scenario, here is what the per acre *ad valorem* charge for the premium would be for these four zones:

Zone	Acreage	Premium	Per Acre
Maximum Impact	200,736	$8,000,000	$39.85
High Impact	468,384	$6,000,000	$12.81
Low Impact	1,003,680	$4,000,000	$3.99
Economic Impact	5,018,400	$2,000,000	$0.40

Now, we must remember that these are *ad valorem* charges and are based on a median per-acre assessed value of $10,000. This means that if a homeowner is in the Maximum Impact Zone and has a one-acre property with an assessed valuation of $1 million that their annual share of the premium would be $3,985. Not pleasant, but certainly not unreasonable for a multi-million dollar home on the beach. On the other hand, if someone owned an acre of pasture in the Appalachian Mountains valued at $2,000, then their "Disaster Tax" would be $0.08. Not bad either.

Seasonal Charges

A seasonal sales tax—charged only during certain months and only in certain coastal counties—is a means of raising revenue from those who enjoy the coasts during those times.

Using Maryland again as an example, the sales tax is 6%. This tax could be raised to 9% from May through September 15, for example, each year. The point here is that places like Ocean City lure visitors from places like Ohio who get the benefit of the beaches, the dunes, the boardwalks, the amusement parks, and even the well-dredged channels so they can launch the boats they tow across country. It is only fair that these folks pay some share of the cost of protecting or rebuilding these facilities. Adding another 3% to the sales tax for the big tourism months will enable these people to help pay.

Maryland's total sales tax collections are approaching $4 billion annually. Le's say that 50% of these taxes are collected between May and October. That's $2 billion. Now, increasing the tax from 6% to 9% is a 50% increase. That means that the May-September sales tax collections should go from $2 billion to $3 billion. That's $1 billion a year to help Maryland pay for these coastal resiliency projects. Assuming $1 billion is much more than is needed, the tax could be further narrowed by having it charged only in specific counties that benefit from their location on or near the coast.

Will the imposition of a seasonal sales tax create howls from the tax-paying Maryland public? Yes, BUT. And the "but" is because sales taxes are deductible from income taxes. So, the extra sales tax they have to pay will be offset by larger income tax deductions. That won't stop the howling completely; but it will certainly dampen it.

Targeted Geographic or Zonal Charges

These are charges that Maryland could impose to help out-of-staters pay their share of coastal resilience costs. For example, there are about 30 million cars that cross the Chesapeake Bay Bridge each year. Let's say that only 10% (three million) of these cars are from out-of-state. The state could impose an additional $3 toll on out-of-state cars. They could easily do this especially with E-Z pass. That would raise $9 million *a year* to help pay for coastal resiliency projects.

Maryland and Virginia could do the same on the Nice Bridge over the lower Bay. Delaware and New Jersey could do the same with the ferryboats between the two states. New York could do this on Long Island. Same with the ferries to Nantucket, Martha's Vineyard, and the like. There is also voluminous precedent for these targeted charges. In many communities, the use of public parks, or parking at public parks, requires a permit, which is free to local residents, but must be paid for by non-residents.

States will, over time, be required to shoulder more of the burden of paying for coastal resilience. The above strategies are food for thought as to how they might do so.

The next few pages will deal with a special legal mechanism to facilitate the protection of vulnerable coastal areas. It is called an interstate compact. It should be noted that an interstate compact could also be a valuable legal mechanism to promote cybersecurity, which is covered later in this chapter.

On August 29, 2005, Hurricane Katrina blew ashore south of New Orleans. The dike and levee system on the lower Mississippi River failed. In all, over 1,800 people died and over $100 billion of damage was done. It was the most devastating storm to hit the United States since 1928.

Help for Katrina's victims in Louisiana and Mississippi came from all over the country. The numbers reported by the National Emergency Management Association are impressive:

- *More than 1,300 search-and-rescue personnel from 16 states searched more than 22,300 structures and rescued 6,582 people.*
- *More than 2,000 healthcare professionals from 28 states treated more than 160,000 patients in the days and weeks after the storms under the most primitive of conditions.*
- *Nearly 3,000 fire/hazmat personnel from 28 states deployed.*
- *Two hundred engineers from nine states assisted.*
- *More than 6,880 sheriff's deputies and police officers from 35 states and countless local jurisdictions deployed across Louisiana and Mississippi—a total of 35% of all of the resources deployed.[1]*

How were all of these resources marshaled? It couldn't have been haphazard or spontaneous.

In fact, this help arrived on the scene thanks to an interstate agreement adopted in 1996 called the Emergency Management Assistance Compact (EMAC).

The last paragraph of Article I, Section 10 of the U.S. Constitution says: "No State shall, without the Consent of Congress . . . enter into any Agreement or Compact with another State, or with a Foreign Power. . . ."

There are some 176 interstate compacts. The first predates the U.S. Constitution. It is the Maryland and Virginia Boundary Agreement of 1785, regulating the Potomac River. This compact was based on Section 2 of Article VI of the Articles of Confederation and Perpetual Union, the language of which was later taken into the Constitution. Interstate compacts require not only the consent of Congress, they also require that each participating state enact a statute incorporating the compact language, and that such legislation be approved by the state's governor.

Typically the process will begin by one of more states passing legislation authorizing a commission to negotiate with another state on a certain issue. Each respective state wishing to involve itself will, in turn, create its own commission. The commissioners will then meet. If they can agree on the substance of an interstate compact, then they will each report back to their respective legislatures with the draft compact which will be put to a vote. If they can't agree, the matter just ends there.

---

1. *See* Emergency Management Assistance Compact, *EMAC Response*, https://www.emacweb.org/index.php/component/content/article/133-training/category-84-b0.html.

Chapter 10: Resilience and Cybersecurity

Once the respective states have adopted the requisite statutes authorizing the compact, they will petition the Congress—presumably through their respective congressional delegations—for its "consent."

There are 54 signatories to the EMAC, including all 50 states, the District of Columbia, Puerto Rico, the Virgin Islands, and Guam. The Compact sets forth the legal framework for interstate cooperation during an emergency. It is, essentially, a mutual aid agreement among the signatories.

The Compact itself does not presume to set forth "how" the mutual aid will be furnished. Those strategies are left to state emergency management officials who work together through the National Emergency Management Association. Rather, the Compact sets out the structure of the relationship between the state being aided and those states furnishing the aid.

The triggering event for calling the Compact into play is the declaration of a state of emergency by a state governor.[2]

The last three paragraphs of "Article III: State Party Responsibilities" describe the specific purposes of the compact:

> v. Protect and assure uninterrupted delivery of services, medicines, water, food, energy and fuel, search and rescue, and critical lifeline equipment, services, and resources, both human and material.
>
> vi. Inventory and set procedures for the interstate loan and delivery of human and material resources, together with procedures for reimbursement or forgiveness.
>
> vii. Provide, to the extent authorized by law, for temporary suspension of any statutes or ordinances that restrict the implementation of the above responsibilities.

Article IV provides:

> Each party state shall afford to the emergency forces of any party state, while operating within its state limits under the terms and conditions of this compact, the same powers (except that of arrest unless specifically authorized by the receiving state), duties, rights, and privileges as are afforded forces of the state in which they are performing emergency services. Emergency forces will continue under the command and control of their regular leaders, but the organizational units will come under the operational control of the emergency services authorities of the state receiving assistance.

---

2. EMAC Art. IV, *available at* https://www.emacweb.org/index.php/learn-about-emac/emac-legislation.

Article V provides that those working under licenses or permits in the state providing aid are deemed duly licensed or permitted in the receiving state, unless the receiving state says otherwise.

Article VI provides that those officers and employees of the providing state are deemed agents of the receiving state "for tort liability and immunity purposes."

Article VII provides that the states providing aid shall pay their own people, including any death benefits.

Article IX says that the receiving state shall reimburse the state providing the aid unless the providing state declines reimbursement.

In addition to EMAC, there is another interstate compact that deals solely with earthquakes: the Interstate Earthquake Emergency Compact. There are, however, only four signatory states. They are Missouri, Indiana, Mississippi, and Tennessee. One would intuitively think that the Pacific Rim states would be the most likely participants in this compact; but, in fact, the largest earthquake in American history occurred in New Madrid, Missouri, on December 16, 1811.

The EMAC can be characterized as a "first responder" agreement. Its purpose is to provide immediate assistance for victims of major emergencies. That said, are there other needs—other than first responder needs—that could be addressed by an agreement among states?

For probably the last several thousand years, tropical waves, otherwise known as "African Easterly Waves," have been forming off the west coast of Africa caused by pulses of intense heat coming off the Sahara Desert. Trade winds blow these phenomena into the Western Hemisphere where some of them intensify into tropical storms and hurricanes.

In 2012, one of these waves spawned Hurricane Sandy, which killed 286 people in 7 countries and caused $68 billion of damage, the second most costly storm in U.S. history after Katrina.

Sandy had winds measured at 115 miles per hour at its peak, which made it a Category 3 Hurricane. When it came ashore in New Jersey it was only a Category 2 storm. What was shocking about Sandy was not its intensity, but its size. Its winds spanned 1,100 miles. The communities in its path were hammered for hours on end. Winds drove high water relentlessly ashore. Whole areas of Manhattan, like Alphabet City, were inundated. The subways in the Wall Street area were flooded out up to their roof tops!

Scientists tell us that the more our planet warms, the more we can expect extreme weather events. In addition, the more the earth warms, the higher

Chapter 10: Resilience and Cybersecurity 93

sea levels will increase. This means that coastal areas face a double jeopardy of more extreme weather events pushing ever-higher seas at them.

The final causative link in this chain of potential disaster is the widespread political belief that the annual appropriations for the Corps, who build many of the coastal fortifications against storms like Sandy, will dwindle over time.

How could an interstate agreement or compact among states help this situation?

There are three concepts that prophesy a role for interstate cooperation. The first concept involves what might be called pre-hurricane fortifications.

Three of the Corps' traditional coastal chores have been the replenishment of beaches, the building of dunes, and the dredging of channels and back bays. All three have vital roles in mitigating the damage of coastal storms.

Beaches erode. So do dunes. Inlets and back bays silt up. Historically the Corps has always scheduled areas for work up and down the coast. These "schedules," however, are for budgetary purposes. Erosion and silting don't depend on congressional calendars. They are caused by wind and currents, which change day-to-day and certainly year-to-year. The rule of thumb is that most beaches need to be replenished every four years. But several years ago Ocean City, Maryland, was hit by a local, but intense, storm that ruined their beaches – within less than a year of their last replenishment.

Now, let us hypothesize that in a day of $0 appropriations for the Corps, Ocean City had squirreled away 25% of the cost of replenishment. What good would that have done them? None. They still would have been short 75% of the money they needed for an "emergency" replenishment. But how would that situation be different if each community from Narragansett to Virginia Beach had all put their 25% into a common kitty. In that case, Ocean City could have gone to the kitty and got the 75% they were out, and paid it back over the next three years.

The second concept is the need to restart a community's economic engine *immediately* after a disaster, as was discussed above.

As we said, people travel to Ocean City from Ohio to walk on the beach, to walk on the boardwalk, to buy French fries and flip-flops on the boardwalk, and to go to the amusement park and other recreational facilities in the city. They do not come from Ohio to shop at Walmart. They don't come from Ohio to visit Ocean City's churches or libraries. So, if the city's beaches, boardwalk, and amusement parks are destroyed, no one is going to come from Ohio until they're rebuilt. These are the essential economic engines or CEDs of Ocean City that have to be rebuilt *yesterday*. This means no grant applications. No approval processes. No inspection visits from federal officials. No Federal Emergency Management Agency. No ceremonies. No waiting. What it does mean is cash available *the day after the disaster* for the mayor and the Ocean City Council to start letting contracts to rebuild the beaches, the boardwalk, all of the flip-flop stores and French fry emporia on the boardwalk, and all of the amusement facilities—all of the facilities that lure Ohioans to their city. No CEDs, no attractions, no tourists. No tourists, no jobs. No jobs, no Ocean City.

How much money is involved in rebuilding a place like Ocean City? It is very difficult to determine from published damage reports. For example, New York and New Jersey report over 650,000 homes damaged by Sandy. If the average damage was $20,000, then the total damage to homes was about $13 billion, or about 20% of the total. According to the U.S. Department of Commerce, 19,000 small businesses in New Jersey sustained damages of over $250,000 for a total of $8.3 billion. How many of these were CEDs is not known.

Of the $42 billion of damage New York says it sustained, about $14 billion in the business and infrastructure areas—the two categories most relevant to resiliency. That is about 25% of the total. Let us, therefore, assume that 40% of this amount, or 10% of the total hurricane damage was to critical facilities. In the case of Hurricane Sandy, that would be about $7 billion. As far as catastrophe insurance and reinsurance are concerned, that is a very reasonable and doable number. Furthermore, since Sandy was the second most destructive storm in history, we can probably prudently estimate that $5 billion should cover most severe weather events.

The third concept that seems to be operating here is that—looking at the Mid-Atlantic coast—a Sandy-like storm can't have a direct hit on every community between Rhode Island and Virginia Beach. This is like saying that out of a fleet of 100 trucks, not all of them will crash this year. In other words, this large spread of geography—Rhode Island to Virginia—in insurance parlance—spells spread of risk; specifically: insurable risk.

How could such insurance work? Let's take pretty little Bethany Beach, Delaware, and Atlantic City, New Jersey, and form an example.

Bethany's post-hurricane needs would be pretty simple: new beach, new boardwalk, some new beachy/touristy shops; that's it. Let us say they might need $10 million, maximum, for all this.

Now, let's take Atlantic City with its massive casinos.[3] Let us say the city thinks it will need another $100 million—over and above the casinos' own insurance to get itself back luring gamblers from Ohio.

---

3. Which we will assume have several billions of their own in catastrophe insurance.

Finally, let's say we have two catastrophe insurance policies (Cat Covers) for the Mid-Atlantic offered through an interstate compact. Policy A has coverage from $1 up to $10 million. Policy B has coverage from $10 million to $100 million. Bethany would buy Policy A only. Atlantic City would buy both.

Insurance drives down the cost of protection. And, insurance is possible because all of the coastal communities buy it, while all of them will not be destroyed by a single event.

So, in summary we have three working concepts: (1) pooling pre-hurricane funds to make sure all communities are well fortified; (2) the immediate rebuilding of the CEDs in communities devastated by disasters; and (3) using catastrophe insurance and reinsurance to pay for rebuilding the CEDs. The pooling in concept #1 and the Cat Covers in concept #3 would require creating agreements among the states. This necessarily means an interstate compact.

In addition, an interstate compact could also facilitate the use of municipal bonds to respond to disasters as well.

Going back to the above example of Bethany Beach, let's say that of the $10 million it thinks it will need to get back into business, $3 million of this—such as the beach itself—is municipal property. Rebuilding the beach would qualify for a tax-exempt bond. In this case, on the one hand, Bethany might opt for a $3 million deductible on its Policy A and plan on funding this $3 million with a tax-exempt bond. On the other hand, issuing so small a tax-exempt bond can be very expensive. On the third hand, having an interstate compact issue a much larger tax-exempt bond on behalf of not only Bethany but also the several other nearby communities that were also devastated by the same storm, might make a great deal of sense. The emergency management officers in each state, who are members of the National Emergency Management Association, should be able to make good sense out of these alternative scenarios. They could thus inform their respective state finance officials who, in turn, could inform their state's representative on the interstate compact.

The compact could well issue the bond in advance and warehouse the funds so that they would literally be on hand the day after the disaster, rather than go through the usual one- to two-month bond issuance process. Again, this is a fiscal decision for the states. But it is the flexibility afforded by the existence of an interstate compact that makes this work.

Suffice it to say there are a myriad of fiscal options that an interstate compact could employ. They can evaluate them all and make their choices for whatever works best for all.

A final note about money. Can states cede away their sovereign control over imposing charges and fees in their own state to an interstate organization? Yes. The Susquehanna River Basin Commission, for example, has a provision in its charter, which enables it to "fix . . . rates . . . charges . . . *without regulation or control by any department, office, or agency of any signatory party*, for . . . any services or products which it provides."[4] On the other hand, however, this goes both ways: the participating states can also severely limit the compacts fiscal powers. Article X of the Port Authority of New York and New Jersey Compact requires that the Authority's board formulate a budget and a work plan each year and then *submit it to the legislatures of both states for approval*. Furthermore, Article XVI authorizes governors *to veto actions of the Authority*. And, in fact, this has actually happened.

So, interstate compacts can be ceded as much, or as little, fiscal authority as their partnering states are comfortable with.

In summary, as the history of the EMAC attests, this legal structure has played a heroic role in protecting human lives and property from disasters. And, it is very likely that this same legal structure can be employed both to protect whole coastal communities from disasters caused by extreme weather events spawned by climate change and to rebuild their core economies the day after disaster strikes. So, innovative financial mechanisms like system benefit charges, seasonal charges, and zonal charges, as well as the innovative use of a major national legal structure like an interstate compact, are what is needed to assure that the country can adapt to and/or mitigate the effects of global warming along its coasts. This is how we can deal with the climate change aspects of "paying for tomorrow."

The next part of this chapter deals with cybersecurity. Please note that an interstate compact dealing with cybersecurity could be a major factor in building a secure, multi-state system for protecting our electric grid.

In his 2014 novel, *Act of War*, a best seller on both the *New York Times* and *USA Today* book lists, American author Brad Thor tells the story of an attack on the United States by China where they use nuclear weapons not to destroy cities or military bases, but rather to create large electro-magnetic pulses (EMPs) that fry our power grids, blacking out all electricity in the country, and bringing the nation to a standstill.

---

4. Susquehanna River Basin Compact §3.9 (emphasis added), *available at* https://www.srbc.net/about/geninfo.htm.

Chapter 10: Resilience and Cybersecurity

An earlier novel, *Warday*, in 1984 told of a similar fate visited on the United States by our then-#1 adversary, the Soviet Union. Oddly enough, the cyberattack is not center stage in *Warday*. Rather it is just part of a larger war that sees major cities and military bases destroyed by nuclear weapons on both sides. Furthermore, the action in *Warday* takes place five years after the war. It is sort of a strange travelogue as two friends travel around the country cataloging war damage and describing how people are adjusting to its aftermath. The major Soviet attack begins with their detonating six nuclear weapons in two triangular patterns over the United States producing electromagnetic pulses that wipe out our power grid and destroy all electrical devices in the country. Thor's book also describes the Chinese strategy of carefully spacing their warheads for maximum destructive impact on our power grid.

EMPs and their destructive capabilities are a very real problem for us. As recently as 2017 the Electric Power Research Institute (EPRI) is doing research on the destruction to the power grid that would be caused by high-altitude EMPs (HEMPs). The HEMPs that EPRI is studying involve the detonation of nuclear weapons high up in the atmosphere, just as Thor wrote about in *Act of War* and authors Whitley Strieber and James Kunetka wrote about in *Warday*.

In addition to foreign governments, terrorists, and hackers, there is an even bigger cyberthreat from one of our neighbors in the galaxy, the sun. In 1859, what has come to be called a "Carrington Event" occurred. Essentially, a storm on the sun threw off massive amounts of EMPs into space. When they struck the earth, they fried all electric power. Now in 1859, the only electricity that existed was used to power telegraphs. So, in 1859, all of the telegraphs went dead. Today, almost everything we do or touch is powered by electricity. If we experience another Carrington Event today, all life on earth could come to a halt.

Enough about EMPs. Suffice it to say that they are one of many threats to our power grid.

In November 2017, the Federal Bureau of Investigation and the U.S. Department of Homeland Security confirmed that the nuclear, aviation, energy, and water sectors, as well as some critical manufacturing industries, had come under cyberattack since at least May of 2017. These attacks have come from foreign governments, terrorists, and professional hackers.

The major problem in responding to this threat is: Who's in charge? Who can give the orders to strengthen this facility or protect that one? The answer is that no one is in charge. There is no central authority that can speak—

much less give orders—to the nuclear, aviation, energy, water and other industries. When it comes to protecting these resources from cyberattacks and other such threats, there needs to be!

So, it is critical that we protect ourselves both from man-made and natural cyberthreats!

To do this, we need a central command. As Americans, we don't think in terms of "central commands" for anything outside of the military. But the cyberthreats we face can hurt us more than any foreign enemy. So, we need an office that can tell each critical sector what it needs to do not only to protect themselves, but also to protect the rest of us who are all interconnected by the power grid.

A "central command" would certainly not be a form of de facto dictatorship. Rather, it could be formed by an agreement among the states and the federal government: an interstate compact. Earlier in this chapter, an interstate compact was discussed as a mechanism for coordinating resilience and mitigation actions among states facing extreme weather events along their seacoasts. An interstate compact could have the same "uniting" role in facing cyberthreats to our grid. In addition to defining a "central command" as the coordinator and director of these protective efforts, the interstate compact would need to vest in the "central command" three specific powers.

First, it needs to raise funds—issue debt—so what needs to get done can get done today - without waiting for taxes or fees to dribble in over time. This debt should carry the most favorable interest rates possible. This means something new in the world of public finance: both a federal guaranty and exemption from all federal and state income taxes. Tax exemption has been enjoyed by municipal bonds issued by states and local governments and agencies for over a century—but never by the federal government. This time has come. This situation is so grave that new ground must be broken. Federally guaranteed debt commands the lowest rates in the international taxable debt market. It will command even lower rates in the tax-exempt market.

Second, this "central command" needs to be a central repository for various fees and taxes that are levied to pay for hardening the grid. Some of the "hardening" should be paid for by federal taxes because it is part of national security. Responding to cyberthreats is every bit as important as fielding a battalion of U.S. Marines. So, some of the money should come out of our taxes. In addition, at least some of the money needs to come from the users of electricity that would disappear in a massive cyberattack. These funds could be part of the electric bills that utilities send out. In this case, the more

Chapter 10: Resilience and Cybersecurity

electricity a customer used, the more he would have to pay to keep it safe. It could also be collected through a national sales tax on electricity bills.

In addition, the companies—like Internet service providers—that absolutely depend on the grid for their survival, should chip in as well. Again, this could either be in the form of surcharges to their customers or as a national sales tax on Internet services.

And third, the "central command" needs to spend these funds (or furnish them to grid participants) where they are needed. There are many poor communities today that cannot pay their water bills. Adding costs for hardening their water system isn't going to work. Someone else needs to pay for it. The point here is that "need" and "money" are not always found in the same place. We need a central authority to distribute funds where they are truly needed.

So protecting ourselves from cyberattacks either from foreign enemies, terrorists, troublemakers, or even Carrington Events, is one of the new, major issues for our generation. It needs coordination and direction across a number of sectors including various levels of government. And we need to create new financing mechanisms to make sure we have the money to get the job done. All of this will be part of "paying for tomorrow."

Resilience and cybersecurity speak to protecting the quality of our lives. Certainly water and air pollution will continue to have a big impact on us. But as global warming continues we will have more extreme weather events. We will need to create resilient systems to protect ourselves and to deal with them. The same is true with cybersecurity. We need to protect ourselves from both natural and manmade events that would severely damage or destroy our electricity grid leaving major parts of the country without power for long periods of time. We need to assure ourselves of a high quality of life in the foreseeable future. And this will definitely involve "paying for tomorrow."

Chapter 11—The Private Sector

Public Private Partnerships are called P3s. P3 is one of the new buzzwords in government. It's like the word "innovative." Everyone in government wants a reputation for being innovative. So, too everyone thinks they can solve intractable problems by throwing P3s at them. This is easier said than done.

A P3 is simply a contract between a public entity, like a government agency, and a private sector organization, like a business, to provide a service to the public. When a village hires a carting company to pick up garbage or leaves in the fall, this is a P3. The F-18 can also be considered a P3 between the McDonnell-Douglas Corporation and the U.S. Navy.

In addition to P3s, the private sector has a major role to play in nutrient credit trading, which will have significant impacts on the financing of nonpoint source pollution control projects. This chapter will deal with both aspects of private-sector participation in the environmental finance business.

A P3 is not a panacea for anything. It isn't a finance mechanism; it is simply a structure for implementing projects. This book is about "paying for tomorrow," so we will examine the financial considerations of dealing with P3s.

The financings for P3s depends on which of the Ps is bringing the money to the party.

If the public P brings the money, then the financing will generally be done through the municipal bond market. This means that the lowest interest rates and the longest possible terms will be available. This means the lowest possible cost for the project.

If the private P brings the money, then it will depend on the private P's appetite for ROI and term or exit strategy, i.e., how fast she wants her money back. If the private P wants an ROI north of 15% and wants out after five years, the project will be very, very expensive. If the private P wants 10% in 10 years, the project will still be very expensive.

To determine whether a P3 might be useful in financing a project we need to categorize projects into two basic classes.

Class A. Projects with no associated income and no realistic possibility of creating a dedicated income stream. Class A projects can be funded in only three ways: (1) gifts from private donors; (2) government grants and legal settlements including compensatory payments; and (3) general obligation bonds, in which case a unit of local government issuing the bond is the donor.

Class B. In terms of identifying funding sources, projects can be further divided by the amount of income they have. As you will see below, projects that are suitable for the (taxable or tax-exempt) municipal bond market provide the lowest interest rates and the longest terms. So, if there's not a lot of income, taxes, or user charges or fees involved, then bonds are a good financing source. If there is substantial project income available, then other financing sources can be explored. They are described below.

P3s can fall into any category. If the private partner is a donor, then it's a Class A project. P3 projects that access the tax-exempt municipal bond market are in Class B1. Class B2 involves getting money from socially responsible investors (SRIs) who put their money where their mouth is, i.e., they are willing to sacrifice some income because of the environmental benefits the project creates.

Class B3 includes investors seeking higher returns and willing to accept higher risks. Private equity funds and hedge funds are examples of these types of investors. It should be noted that public pension funds, sovereign wealth funds, and the like—which one might think to be SRIs—aren't necessarily. The California Public Employees Retirement System (CalPERS) is the largest pension fund in the United States. It has $294 billion of assets; $31.3 billion, or a little over 10% of which, is invested in "private equity." Its benchmark return rate for its private equity investments for the fiscal year ending June 30, 2016 was 15.4%.

The chart on the following page displays the classes of projects with their associated financing sources along with their terms, rates, and ROI:

Chapter 11: The Private Sector

Class	Funding Source	Term (Years)	Annual Rate of Return	Annual Return (Cost) per $1,000
A	Donors/ G.O. Bonds	n/a	0%	n/a
B1	Bond Market	30+	<5%	$65.05
B2	SRI Funds/ Investors	~20	5-10%	$117.46
B3	Private Equity/ Hedge Funds	5-7	15-40%	$240.36 (low) $491.36 (high)

In summary, once we know the type of private partner who is financing the project, we can determine the annual cost of that project to those who must pay for it.

In Chapter 2, we discussed strategies for financing nonpoint source water pollution projects where a single property owner, rather than a water/wastewater utility with a user/customer base of several thousand homes and businesses, will be the one individual undertaking a project, and, hence, will be expected to pay for it. One of these strategies where the private sector can play an important role is in nutrient credit trading. In fact, the private sector will not only play a major role in nutrient trading, in most cases, they will actually be on both sides of the transaction. Private individuals, such as farmers, will undertake projects that generate nutrient credits. Once generated, the farmer will sell the credits. Private individuals, such as real estate developers, will need credits to obtain some of the permits required for their developments; so they will be on the buying end of the nutrient credit trade.

As noted in Chapter 2, although nutrient credit trading could be an important source of financing for nonpoint source pollution control projects, it has not matured enough as a science to be so. Today, several states have some form of nascent nutrient credit trading programs, but they are so-called point-to-point programs. This means, for example, that a utility with an NPDES permit for far more nutrients than it generates can sell the credits for those extra nutrients to another utility that needs them to comply with its own permit. But as far as nonpoint source pollution is concerned, the environmental scientists have not been able to agree on a system of counting credits that is acceptable to all parties involved. So, there the matter lies: a good idea with great, but yet unrealized, potential.

Finally, we can't leave the subject of the private sector without mentioning that the millions of buyers of the municipal bonds that supply the money for over 90% of pollution control projects are themselves the private sector. The size of the municipal bond market is some $3.7 *trillion*. Between $300 and $400 billion of new municipal bonds are issued each year. So, in a sense, the municipal bond market can be considered to be one of the largest, and certainly most successful, P3s on the planet. The municipal bond market will certainly continue to be one of our major means of "paying for tomorrow."

Glossary

ADSPs – annual debt service payments

AMWA – American Municipal Water Association

ASCE – American Society of Civil Engineers

AWWA – American Water Works Association

BMP – best management practice

BRT – bus rapid transport

CAA – Clean Air Act

CalPERS – California Public Employees Retirement System

CAP – customer assistance program

CED – core economic drivers

CIFA – Council of Infrastructure Financing Agencies

CO_2 – carbon dioxide

CWA – Clean Water Act of 1972

CWSRF – Clean Water State Revolving Fund

DBT – declining block tariff

DWSRF – Drinking Water State Revolving Fund

EIA – Energy Information Administration

EMAC – Emergency Management Assistance Compact

EMPs – electro-magnetic pulses

ENR – enhanced nutrient removal

EPA – U.S. Environmental Protection Agency

EPRI – Electric Power Research Institute

ERU – equivalent residential unit

GAO – U.S. Government Accountability Office

GHGs – greenhouse gases

HEMP – high-altitude EMPs

IBT – increasing block tariff

kwh – kilowatt hour

LIHEAP – Low-Income Household Energy Assistance Program

LoC – Letter of Credit

LP – level payment

LPP – level principal payment

MES – Maryland Environmental Service

MHI – median household income

MS4 – municipal separate storm sewer system

NACWA – National Association of Clean Water Administrators

NAWC – National Association of Water Companies

NEPA – National Environmental Policy Act

NPDES – National Pollutant Discharge Elimination System

Glossary

NRWA – National Rural Water Association

OPM – other people's money

P3 – public-private partnership

POTW – publicly owned treatment works

RCRA – Resource Conservation and Recovery Act

RGGI – Regional Greenhouse Gas Initiative

ROI – return on investment

S&P – Standard & Poor's

SBCs – system benefit charges

SDWA – Safe Drinking Water Act of 1974

SFR – Self Funded Reserve

SRF – both the Clean Water State Revolving Fund and the Safe Drinking Water State Revolving Fund

SRI – socially responsible investors

STD – Special Tax District

TRIs – tax revenue intercepts

USDA – U.S. Department of Agriculture

WEF – Water Environment Federation

w/w – water & wastewater

Notes

Notes

Notes

Notes